Cont

INTRODUCTION

REMEMBER the old picture of retirement in America, where grand-parents spent their time sitting on a porch rocker recounting the good old days? Several generations of a family lived together, or close by, and parents and grandparents were cared for during old age by their children or grandchildren.

Today, the picture is vastly different. Most retirees now expect to be financially independent; retired parents usually maintain households separate from their children; and, given the greater geographical mobility that characterizes today's economy, the children of retirees often live far distant from their parents. Pensions, savings, and Social Security have largely replaced the family as the primary source of support in old age. More than in the past, older people are on their own, physically and financially.

The retirement picture is changing yet again for the children and grandchildren of today's senior citizens. As they plan for retirement, they must do so under a different set of assumptions than current retirees:

1. Future retirees cannot count on Social Security to cover as much of their expenses as it does for today's retirees.

2. The percentage of workers covered by pensions is decreasing, and companies that do offer plans increasingly require employees to take the initiative to fund them and decide how they are invested.

3. As a matter of longevity, the retirement years today represent a larger portion of life than ever before. Increases in life expectancy and a trend toward early retirement have resulted in a lower ratio of working years to retirement years. Consequently, there are fewer years in which to accumulate savings for lengthier retirements. Future retirees without sufficient savings may have to work longer.

4. Medical costs are rising faster than prices generally, which means that you must budget today for higher expenses in the future. At the same time, many companies are cutting back on retiree health benefits, leaving coverage gaps that early retirees must address on their own.

Despite these critical issues, it is possible to enjoy a high standard of living in retirement if you plan during the working years to meet the costs of doing so. The purpose of this book is to help you make the most of your opportunities to save for retirement. Today's era of early retirement, longer life expectancies, and independent living can make the retirement years a time for travel, leisure, and fruitful activity — but only if you have prepared prudently beforehand.

ABOUT THE AUTHORS

AMERICAN Institute for Economic Research (AIER) published the original edition of *How to Plan for Your Retirement Years* in 1988. Since then it has gone through a number of editions and benefited from the collective effort of a number of authors. The current edition builds on those earlier efforts and also incorporates the recent findings of other Institute research on investing, estate planning, health care, and elder care that is available in separate AIER publications (see inside back cover for details). This edition was prepared by three individuals:

Kerry A. Lynch is the Director of Research and Education at AIER. She joined the research staff in 1987 and has written widely on economic and personal finance issues. She and Dr. Robert Gilmour, who served as President of AIER, prepared the first edition of this book.

Marla Brill is an AIER Research Associate and the author of the AIER book *How to Give Wisely* and of *Windfall: Managing Unexpected Money So It Doesn't Manage You* (published by Alpha Books). An experienced financial journalist, she has written numerous articles for AIER and for *Kiplinger's Personal Finance* magazine, *Investors' Business Daily*, and other publications.

Dr. R. D. Norton is an AIER Research Associate and was a Visiting Research Fellow at AIER in 1999 and 2006. He has written or edited ten books, starting with a monograph on sales taxes at the Tax Foundation, and including works on city and regional growth and on the entrepreneurial economy. He was formerly Executive Director of the Eastern Economic Association.

I.
RETIREMENT STRATEGIES IN
FINANCIAL PERSPECTIVE

THERE is a simple rule to remember about saving for retirement. Save as much as you can as soon as you are financially able to do so, because the "magic of compounding" is much more powerful over longer periods of time. Consider that if you save $1,000 a year in an account earning eight percent, you will have about $79,000 after 25 years (before taxes). After ten years, using the same assumptions, the balance would be only about $16,000.

Another way to make this same point appears in Table 1, which shows how large a sum even modest monthly savings can generate, if you start early.

Given our culture of consumption, setting aside even modest amounts is often easier said than done. In addition to paying for the necessities of life, people spend money on everything from flat-screen television sets to luxury cars to resort vacations for the family. Saving for retirement is often an afterthought.

In any case, financial priorities will no doubt shift during the course of your income-earning years. At some points, immediate needs such as buying a house or funding a child's education may seem more important than setting aside money for a retirement that may be years, or even decades, away.

Once you meet the primary responsibilities at the various stages of your "financial life," however, you should address your expected retirement needs and decide how to provide for them. One of the best ways to do this is to automatically set aside either a percentage of earnings or a specific dollar amount each month, through payroll deduction at your place of work or through the automatic investment plans offered by many brokers and mutual

---

Table 1: **How Much You Need to Invest to Reach $100,000 at Retirement**

(Savings in a tax-deferred account earning an 8 percent rate of return)

Contributions Made from Age...	Monthly Contribution	Total Contribution
25 to 65	$29	$13,920
30 to 65	$44	$18,480
35 to 65	$67	$24,120
40 to 65	$105	$31,500
45 to 65	$170	$40,800
50 to 65	$289	$52,020
55 to 65	$547	$65,640

fund firms. A systematic saving and investment program changes retirement saving from an afterthought to a regular, fixed expense.

Of course, the amount you are able to contribute will depend in part on your stage in life. From the standpoint of financial responsibilities, most people's lifetimes may be divided into three phases: (1) the earlier working years, (2) the later working years, and (3) the period after retirement.

The Earlier Working Years: Establishing a Base

No matter what your financial responsibilities or age, you should always try to make saving a priority. Your goal should be the continued, uninterrupted funding of a saving plan in an amount you can reasonably afford.

Of course, you will probably be able to save more in some years than in others. During the earlier working years, especially if you are unmarried or without children, your financial responsibilities probably are minimal. There are exceptions, of course, as when a younger single person must help care for aged, disabled, or unemployed parents or others. But usually, young working people focus on immediate needs such as paying debts incurred for schooling or establishing a separate household and accumulating some savings for marriage and a family.

After marriage but before children arrive, a young couple's opportunity to save may increase, particularly if both partners work full time. Savings may take the form of tangible assets (furniture, appliances, vehicles, etc.) and financial assets. The financial assets provide an emergency fund, a temporary portion destined for "big-ticket" purchases, and a longer-term portion for a down payment on a house or condominium. If both spouses are self-supporting, life insurance adequate to cover final expenses and readjustment should be sufficient. Medical insurance is essential to protect against today's high-cost medical care.

The young adult with children may have little money left for investment. Life insurance needs are greatest at this time because parents must provide sufficient coverage to support their children until they become independent, and perhaps provide additional income for the spouse. Providing for education for the children also may have a high priority.

At this stage of life, amounts earmarked for retirement are often minimal or non-existent. Many young householders cannot afford even to carry all the life insurance needed for protection of dependents. An employer may offer a retirement plan, and you should consider this (among perhaps many factors) when accepting or leaving a job. In addition, most working people of any age will be participating in the compulsory Social Security system, through which they earn claims to future benefits. Most people, however,

4

will have to meet insurance and other savings needs before they can develop a long-term investment plan.

The Later Working Years: Stepping Things Up

Many individuals and families can begin a significant effort to save once they reach their peak earning years, particularly if their children have become financially independent. With family costs and insurance needs reduced, this later working period for many people provides the best opportunity to accumulate assets for retirement.

Once you turn 50, the tax laws encourage increased tax-deferred saving. Under the "catch-up" provisions of the federal income tax code, limits on tax-deferred contributions to 401(k)-type accounts and Individual Retirement Accounts are raised.

Such tax incentives for increased saving figure prominently in the "Timeline for Retirement" featured in a recent U.S. Department of Labor publication on retirement planning[1]:

"At age 50	Begin making catch-up contributions….
At 59½,	No more tax penalties on early withdrawals from retirement accounts….
At 62	The minimum age to receive Social Security benefits….
At 65	Eligible for Medicare.
At 66	Eligible for full Social Security benefits if born between 1943 and 1954.
At 70½	Start taking minimum withdrawals from most retirement accounts…."

At this time, the prospect of retirement becomes a principal factor in investment and employment decisions. In many cases, investors nearing retirement should avoid high-risk investments because they may have neither the time nor the individual financial resources to recover financially from a major loss. The prospective retiree must consider whether expected Social Security and benefits will be sufficient to meet retirement needs, whether early retirement is desirable and affordable, and how much additional saving is needed to provide an adequate standard of living in retirement.

Measuring Your Retirement Readiness

There is abundant evidence that many people over 55 have not set aside

---

[1] Source: U.S. Department of Labor, *Taking the Mystery Out of Retirement Planning*, 2006.

enough savings to be comfortable or confident of retiring "on schedule" at 62, 65, or even later. While their goal may be to build a nest egg that will support a certain standard of living in retirement, they are falling short and have few years to make up the shortfall. The options in this scenario are (1) to keep working, full or part-time, in one's later years; (2) to scale back one's idea of an acceptable retirement standard of living; or (3) both.

To be sure, many seniors would prefer to work, for reasons of social satisfaction or intrinsic interest, even if they could afford a life of complete leisure. But some believe they must work out of economic necessity, while others find that, for medical or other reasons, they are no longer able to work.

In this context, you face a number of pre-retirement scenarios, but they boil down to two issues: whether you have an adequate nest egg *and* whether you have the option to keep working. One scenario is that you find yourself with enough money to retire and a job that you like and can continue to do. Another is that you reach retirement age without enough money to retire and without job prospects. Needless to say, the latter situation is best avoided.

Your Retirement Strategy: What Comes Next

In retirement planning as in the business world, a strategy can be thought of as a plan for success in a hostile or uncertain environment. To help you enter retirement on your own terms, this book covers the essentials of retirement planning and finance.

Only you can decide the right strategy for yourself and your family. But one crucial step in that direction is likely to be determining the size of the nest egg you will need once you stop working—and how much monthly saving it will take to get you there. This is the subject of the next chapter. Following that, Chapter III considers the related issue of planning for life's contingencies, the big and little surprises and reversals that can derail your retirement savings plan. Subsequent chapters consider Social Security, pensions, 401(k)s, IRAs, and investment issues.

The next step, then, is to identify your future financial needs and likely sources of future income.

II.
ESTIMATING YOUR
RETIREMENT SAVINGS GOAL

EVEN though there are many years to plan for it, saving for retirement frequently catches people off guard, as more immediate demands on income may crowd out a plan for saving. At the same time, for a variety of reasons saving for retirement has become more urgent than ever in recent years.

But just how much saving is required, given your circumstances?

Unfortunately, there is no foolproof way to answer this question. The future purchasing power of the dollar is highly uncertain, and with it the purchasing power of any pension payments you may receive. Nor is it easy to predict the rate of return on your savings. Meantime, the prospect of a traditional, fixed-benefit pension is itself fast-fading into the sunset, so that more and more of the responsibility for saving is being shifted to the employee.

Nevertheless, even a rough estimate of retirement savings requirements seems preferable to remaining completely in the dark. Accordingly, we now describe how a savings plan, begun at a given age, can be designed to fund a specific retirement income.

It must be emphasized at the outset that the illustrations we will provide in this chapter are only a first approximation offering general guidelines as to how much you will want to save each month. In essence, the answer is, the more saving the better. If you save too much, the worst thing that will happen is that you will leave a larger estate.

First, we review a number of factors to consider in estimating how large your post-retirement income should be to maintain your standard of living.

Estimating Your Retirement Expenses

Your expenses after retirement may differ substantially from those in your working years. The net effect for most people is that a smaller income—perhaps much smaller—can maintain your standard of living after retirement.

There are several reasons to expect expenses to go down. First, a large part of the family budget before retirement is devoted to raising children, who, if all goes well, will be financially independent by the time you retire. Second, work-related expenses, such as commuting, clothing, etc.,

7

also will be lower. Third, mortgages may be paid off by this time. Fourth, once you reach retirement age you may be in a position to stop "saving for retirement."

Finally, your tax bill may also diminish upon retirement. For many retirees, taxable income drops substantially. Depending on total income levels, Social Security benefits may be either tax-free or only proportionally taxed. Annuity income that represents return of principal is not taxed. Except for tax-sheltered retirement plans—such as 401(k)s—savings withdrawn to meet current expenses are not deemed "income" for tax purposes.

Moreover, Federal tax law provides a higher standard deduction for taxpayers aged 65 or older who do not itemize. In 2005, the "additional standard deduction" was $1,250 for single taxpayers. For those who were married filing jointly, married filing separately, or a qualifying widow or widower, the additional amount was $1,000. State tax codes often provide similar deductions for the aged.

In addition, in many states "homestead exemptions" for property taxes allow seniors to pay lower property taxes on their homes. Nor are such exemptions trivial. In one western state, for example, a home with an assessed value of $300,000 qualifying for the homestead exemption incurs a tax liability of $520, rather than $3,500. At the Federal level, a homeowner is entitled to exclude from taxation up to $250,000 ($500,000 for married couples filing jointly) of the capital gain on the sale of a principal home.

Since your tax status may change considerably upon retirement, it may be worthwhile to consult a tax planner to ensure you are taking full advantage of the privileges of age accorded you by the IRS and by state and local governments.

By contrast, *medical expenditures* can be expected to increase. These increases may partially offset the reductions in expenditures noted above. True, Medicare becomes available at 65, but it is only a partial shield against rising health costs. This issue is too complicated to try to summarize here. Suffice it to say that some recent analyses come up with a current out-of-pocket estimate of medical expenses after 65 of about $3,500 a year—and rising.

Similarly, at-home care costs may also rise in later years. Such costs may include not only at-home health care, but a variety of home-maintenance and other services as well.

At bottom, health care and home care expenses in retirement are unpredictable. There is always the possibility that they will be very large. While it is hard to budget for unpredictable situations (few of us know what our health or personal circumstances will be 10 or 20 years from now), it is

8

important to keep in mind that health-driven changes can become—gradually or suddenly—a major factor in your finances after you retire.

Figuring Out Your "Replacement" Income

The net effect for most people is that costs of living go down after retirement, at least initially, so a "replacement rate" of less than 100 percent of your pre-retirement income may be adequate. (A replacement rate is your gross income after retirement, expressed as a percentage of your income before retirement.) In other words, it typically takes a lower income after retirement to maintain the same standard of living, for the reasons just described.

How much lower depends on many factors, most notably your pre-retirement income. The Aon Consulting Group and a team of Georgia State University researchers have studied the question of how much recommended replacement rates vary with income. Using data from the federal government's Consumer Expenditure Survey, they periodically estimate the replacement rates that retirees, both individuals and couples, need at different income levels in order to maintain their pre-retirement standard of living.

Their latest (2004) estimates were based on spending profiles of about 15,000 households, some still working and some after retirement. As indicated in Table 2, at first the necessary replacement rate goes down as income rises. For married couples, it falls to 75 percent at $60,000. In other words, a couple with a gross income of $60,000 before retirement would typically need an income of $45,000 after retirement to maintain their standard of living. Above that income, however, the needed replacement rate begins to rise, approaching 80 percent at $90,000.

Table 2: **How Much Of Your Working Income Will You Need After Retirement?**

Pre-retirement Income (2004 Dollars)	Recommended Replacement Rates to Maintain Standard of Living	
	Single	Married
$20,000	82%	89%
30,000	79	84
40,000	76	80
50,000	74	77
60,000	74	75
70,000	78	76
80,000	81	77
90,000	82	78

Source: The Aon Consulting/Georgia State University *2004 Retirement Income Replacement Ratio Study*.

9

Chart 1 shows why 75 percent is the recommended replacement ratio for a pre-retirement income of $60,000. First, federal taxes usually fall sharply once you stop working. Second, age-related cost reductions for large non-medical budget items (such as mortgages) often outweigh rising medical and other age-related expenses. Third, you no longer need to allocate part of your income to "saving for retirement."

However, above a retirement income of $45,000, federal income taxes kick in again. As a result, it takes more pre-tax income in retirement to match the pre-retirement standard of living. Above a retirement income of about $45,000, in short, rising income taxes can boost the needed replacement rate from 75 percent to higher ratios.

This study suggests that, to be on the safe side, replacement rates ranging from 75 to 90 percent should be adequate for most people to maintain pre-retirement standards of living.

On the other hand, you are not a statistic. You do have your own personal

Chart 1: **How $45,000 in Retirement Income Can Replace $60,000 of Pre-Retirement Income**

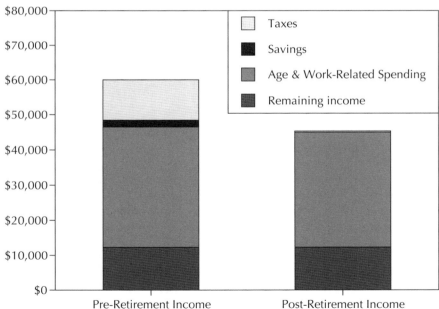

Source: Based on data in The Aon Consulting/Georgia State University *2004 Retirement Income Replacement Ratio Study*, p. 2.

circumstances and preferences to consider.

For one thing, relatively higher annual earnings during the few years im-mediately preceding retirement may overstate the level of income needed to maintain current living standards. To that extent, an average of your annual earnings during the 10 years or so before retirement may be more representative of your pre-retirement income.

More subjectively, if you are in good health and have a willingness to ex-periment, you can find new lifestyles (or, better said, "consumption styles") that can allow you to get by on less income than any of these comparisons suggest. The notion of a rigid or inflexible replacement rate assumes that you want your retirement lifestyle to resemble that of your working years. You may well imagine other possibilities. If so, you may manage to get by on a much lower income (say, 40 percent of your working-age income, not 75) to provide you with an equivalent sense of well-being and security.

Sources of Income

The point so far is that once you calculate your pre-retirement income, you can use a replacement rate to estimate the income you will need in retire-ment. If the average of your 10 years of income from 55 to 65 is $60,000, a replacement rate of 75 percent is in order, implying a target income in retirement of $45,000.

Once you have estimated how much income you will need in retirement, you then must figure out where it will come from. Social Security benefits alone are unlikely to be enough for many people, particularly those with high earnings. The Social Security Administration estimates that benefits currently replace less than one-fourth of the earnings of a worker who earned the maximum subject to Social Security tax throughout his life-time (for 2007, the maximum is $97,500). However, few workers earned this maximum wage every year. For the majority, Social Security benefits typically will replace a larger portion of earnings. Indeed, the lower your wages, the larger the portion of your pre-retirement income that Social Security replaces.

Higher-income workers nearing retirement are more likely to be covered by pensions and more likely to be able to have built up a reliable nest egg. Of course, the fading of fixed-benefit pension plans over the past decade has made this source of retirement income much less common than it was a generation ago. Still, some workers nearing retirement—especially those working in the public sector—can count pensions among their sources of retirement income. Others will have built up their own savings through 401(k) or IRA accounts. Indeed, these individual accounts are key compo-nents of the nest egg you will want to build.

According to a 2006 report from the Social Security Administration, for the elderly population as a whole the aggregate percentages of retirement income provided by various sources in 2004 were:

Source	Percentage
Social Security	39
Earnings from work	26
Pensions	19
Assets	12
Other	4

These amounts represent only statistical aggregates. Individual circumstances will differ. We have provided these figures only as a rough illustration of what some current retirees have experienced, and they may be of some use in your own planning if no other information is available. However, you are advised to estimate as accurately as possible sources of your own income based on your individual circumstances.

How large will your Social Security benefit be? Every year the Social Security Administration sends workers and former workers aged 25 and older an updated estimate of their benefits. If you do not receive yours in the mail, or want another copy, you can get one by phoning Social Security at 1-800-772-1213 and requesting a "Personal Earnings and Benefit Estimate Statement." A calculator located at the administration's website (www.ssa.gov) can also help you figure your benefit.

If you participate in a traditional, fixed-benefit pension plan, you may be able to get an estimate of pension income from your employer.

To give you an idea of how to put all this information together, Table 3

Table 3: **Estimate of Savings Needed to Fund Equivalent Retirement Income at Selected Income Levels**

(1) ×	(2) =	(3)	(4)	(5)	(6)	(7)
Preretire-ment Income	Replace-ment Rate	Equivalent Retirement Income	— — Amount Provided by: — — Social Security	Pensions	Earnings and Assets	Unadjusted Assets Needed
$20,000	0.89	$17,800	$13,000	$3,400	$1,400	$35,000
30,000	0.84	25,200	16,800	4,800	3,600	90,000
40,000	0.80	32,000	20,400	6,100	5,500	137,000
50,000	0.77	38,500	24,000	7,300	7,200	180,000
60,000	**0.75**	**45,000**	**25,800**	**8,600**	**10,600**	**265,000**
70,000	0.76	53,200	27,300	10,100	15,800	395,000
80,000	0.77	51,600	28,000	11,700	21,900	547,500
90,000	0.78	70,200	29,700	13,500	27,000	675,000

shows hypothetical retirement income sources for a number of different pre-retirement income levels. Column (1) shows pre-retirement income, reflecting the assumed average gross income of the 10 years before retirement. To estimate your income needs in retirement, you can use the replacement rates listed in Column (2). Multiplying the entries in the first column by the entries in the second gives you the equivalent retirement income, as listed in Column (3).

Estimating the Nest Egg

The next step is to identify how much more, if anything, you need to save to build a nest egg sufficient to pay for your retirement.

Possible sources of expected income appear in columns (4), (5), and (6). These are not necessarily "typical" amounts, but are instead based simply on the aggregates listed earlier for all Social Security retirement beneficiaries in a recent year. On this basis, they list income that would come from Social Security, pensions, and personal earnings and assets.

In place of these hypothetical figures, you are advised to make more realistic estimates based on the specifics of your retirement provisions. For example, *if you do not have a defined-benefit pension plan, you should leave out the figure for column (5).*

How big a nest egg will you need? To begin to derive an answer, column (6), "Earnings and Assets," shows the gap after Social Security and pension income have been deducted from the retirement income amounts shown in column (3). The amounts in column (6) thus show income that must come from either savings or "post-retirement" employment earnings.

In this discussion we assume that the entire amount required must come from savings. The reason is that while some seniors will want to keep a hand in a business or profession, many others are physically not capable of active work. For planning purposes, therefore, it is prudent not to have to depend on employment earnings in retirement.

The last item, column (7), shows the total amount of assets needed to provide the income flow shown in column (6). Rather than using complicated formulas here, we shall rely on a rule of thumb to provide a good approximation of the nest egg to target.

The rule of thumb provides a conservative rate for you to tap into your nest egg. To be specific, this rate—used in various financial planning software models—suggests *an initial withdrawal of only about four percent of your nest egg* at 65. Then each year you assume that you withdraw the same amount, adjusted upward for price inflation. This four-percent rule is viewed as a conservative approach that would minimize the risk that you would outlive your savings.

A corollary of the four-percent withdrawal rule is that for any given income component beyond a pension and Social Security, the required nest egg at retirement is 25 times as large. Given the gap, in short, multiply it by 25 to find the nest egg you need.

As an example from Table 3, a person moving from a pre-retirement income of $60,000 to a replacement income of $45,000 has to fill an income gap of $10,600. The question is, four percent of what initial nest egg equals $10,600? The answer turns out to be 25 times the needed $10,600, or $265,000.[1]

The same multiple can be applied to the income gaps and required nest eggs at other income levels in Table 3. Whatever the annual income gap after taking into account Social Security and any traditional pension benefits, multiply it by 25 to find the required sum. To be clear: there is no guarantee that this sum will be sufficient for your retirement. But it gives you a ballpark figure to work with.

Converting the Gap Estimate to a Monthly Savings Plan

Now you need to convert your estimate of required savings into a systematic savings plan. Table 4 lists the "savings factors" that give the amounts to be saved annually if the retirement program is to be fully funded. We list them based on assumed returns on savings of three, five, and seven percent per year. The lower the rate of return, of course, the higher the amount you will have to save each month to meet a specified savings goal.

The example above gave $265,000 as a target nest egg. If you are now 50, this is the amount that must be attained by the time you reach age 65. To find out how much to save each year, multiply this amount by one of the annual savings factors for a 50-year-old listed in Table 4. If we assume an average investment return of seven percent per year, for example, the corresponding savings factor for a 50-year old is .037. Multiplying $265,000 x .037 gives an annual savings requirement of $9,805, or about $820 a month.

Note that if you are now 40 years old, you would need to set aside far less: $3,975 per year, or about $330 per month. This underscores the benefit of setting aside savings as early as you can and letting the "miracle of compounding" help you reach your goal.

---

[1] From high-school algebra, we want to find the amount for the variable NEST-EGG, such that .04(NESTEGG) = $10,600. Dividing both sides by .04, we get NESTEGG = $10,600/.04 or $265,000. Dividing the number $10,600 by four percent (.04) to get the nest egg amount is the same as multiplying $10,600 by (1/.04), and (1/.04) = 25.

To recap, you can estimate your target nest egg at the beginning of your retirement (at age 65) by multiplying your estimated income gap by 25. Then you can find the annual savings needed to reach this goal by multiplying the target nest egg by an annual savings factor from one of the three columns in Table 4.

Given your age, you can assume different investment rates of return to estimate how much you need to save annually to reach that goal. The worksheets at the end of this chapter may help in your calculations.

Using an Online Calculator To Test Your Plan's Adequacy

A valuable self-help tool for thinking about your retirement plan is a retirement calculator, as offered on various online websites, such as www.dinkytown.com. You will be asked to provide data about your age,

Table 4: **Annual Savings Factors**

Age	Assuming Annual Investment Yield is:		
	3%	*5%*	*7%*
40	0.027	0.020	0.015
41	0.028	0.021	0.016
42	0.030	0.023	0.017
43	0.032	0.025	0.019
44	0.034	0.027	0.021
45	0.036	0.029	0.023
46	0.039	0.031	0.025
47	0.041	0.034	0.027
48	0.045	0.037	0.030
49	0.048	0.040	0.034
50	0.052	0.044	0.037
51	0.057	0.049	0.041
52	0.062	0.054	0.046
53	0.068	0.060	0.052
54	0.076	0.067	0.059
55	0.085	0.076	0.068
56	0.096	0.086	0.078
57	0.109	0.100	0.091
58	0.127	0.117	0.108
59	0.150	0.140	0.131
60	0.183	0.172	0.163
61	0.232	0.221	0.210
62	0.314	0.302	0.291
63	0.478	0.465	0.451
64	0.971	0.952	0.935
65	1.000	1.000	1.000

savings, preferred retirement age, marital status, and the like. Once you enter these and a few other numbers (including assumed rates of price inflation and returns on investments), the calculator will map out a trajectory for your retirement account to test its adequacy.

Here is an example from dinkytown.com for a person 9 years away from retirement who provided the following data:

Current age	56	*Household income*	$100,000
Rate of return before retirement	6%	*Age of retirement*	65
Rate of return during retirement	5%	*Expected salary rise*	0%
Years until retirement	9	*Years of retirement*	25
Percent of income at retirement	80%	*Current savings*	$500,000
Percent of income to contribute	8%	*Expected inflation*	3.1%
Your last year's income	$100,000	*Retirement budget*	$80,000
Include Social Security?	"Yes"	*Are you married?*	"Yes"

The conclusion that pops out on the website for these numbers: "Your ending balance is $89,585." Under the assumptions entered above, the accumulated savings at the age of 65 plus Social Security benefits would pay an annual income (adjusted for inflation) of $80,000 for 25 years. At that point, in the dry language of the calculator site, you "end" your retirement, leaving a balance for your heirs of about $90,000.

Chart 2 and Table 5 illustrate the logic behind this estimate. For the hypothetical individual in the chart, retirement savings peak when he is 65 (at $877,000). At this point he stops earning income from employment—and he is assumed to stop saving for retirement. Meantime he begins drawing Social Security. Given his high lifetime earnings and his marital status, he is projected to receive the maximum estimated benefit of just over $37,000.

The replacement rate of income we have entered in this example is 80 percent of his last year's salary, which works out to $80,000. In round numbers the gap between his desired retirement income and his Social Security payments is $43,000 (or $80,000 - $37,000). In his first year of retirement, at 65, that gap is filled by a withdrawal from his retirement account of the same amount.

Each year thereafter, until his assumed death at 90, his spending and his Social Security payment are assumed to go up apace with inflation (assumed to be 3.1 percent per year). The amount that must bridge the gap between the two is filled by a withdrawal from the pool of retirement savings. According to this simulation, "Your plan is on track." That means that his retirement savings will carry him through to the age of 90, with something left over.

What if Something Goes Wrong?

Of course any number of things could interfere with this rosy scenario. It is based on a multitude of assumptions that may not prove accurate. We can focus on three of the most likely pitfalls: higher inflation, the need for long-term care, and outliving the plan.

What if the assumed rate of price inflation is too low? The rate we entered into the calculator, 3.1 percent a year, is the rate suggested on the website, because that was the average rate from 1925 to 2005. Others would suggest a rate of 3.5 percent, roughly the average for the last few years. But even that might be too low, if only because medical costs have recently been increasing twice as fast (seven percent a year) as the general price level, and Medicare may not shield you fully. In that case, your expenses could well rise more rapidly, straining your budget.

Chart 2: **A 25-Year Retirement Simulation**

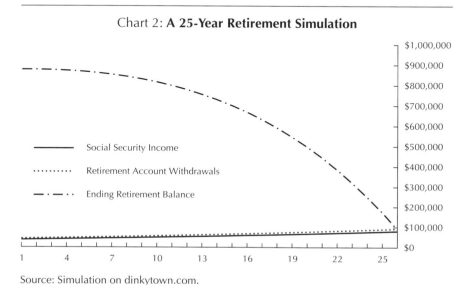

Source: Simulation on dinkytown.com.

17

Second, the plan has made no provision for long-term care, as in an assisted-living facility, a nursing home, or in your own home. Since current annual costs of nursing-home care average $73,000 nationwide (and range much higher in some regions), a severe disability can throw otherwise prudent plans into disarray. This long-term care contingency is discussed more fully in the next chapter. In brief, the point suggested there is that recent changes in Medicaid law make *long-term-care insurance* a more attractive feature of a retirement plan than in the past.

Table 5: **25-Year Retirement Simulation**

Age	Beginning Retirement Balance	Investment Growth	Contributions: 8% of Income	Retire with 80% of Income	Social Security Income	Retirement Account Withdrawals	Ending Retirement Balance
57	$500,000	$30,000	$8,000	$0	$0	$0	$538,000
58	538,000	32,280	8,000	0	0	0	578,280
59	578,280	34,697	8,000	0	0	0	620,977
60	620,977	37,259	8,000	0	0	0	666,235
61	666,235	39,974	8,000	0	0	0	714,210
62	714,210	42,853	8,000	0	0	0	765,062
63	765,062	45,904	8,000	0	0	0	818,966
64	818,966	49,138	8,000	0	0	0	876,104
65	876,104	43,805	0	80,000	37,227	42,773	877,136
66	877,136	43,857	0	82,480	38,381	44,099	876,894
67	876,894	43,845	0	85,037	39,571	45,466	875,273
68	875,273	43,764	0	87,673	40,798	46,875	872,162
69	872,162	43,608	0	90,391	42,063	48,328	867,442
70	867,442	43,372	0	93,193	43,367	49,826	860,988
71	860,988	43,049	0	96,082	44,711	51,371	852,666
72	852,666	42,633	0	99,061	46,097	52,964	842,336
73	842,336	42,117	0	102,131	47,526	54,605	829,847
74	829,847	41,492	0	105,297	48,999	56,298	815,041
75	815,041	40,752	0	108,562	50,518	58,043	797,750
76	797,750	39,887	0	111,927	52,084	59,843	777,794
77	777,794	38,890	0	115,397	53,699	61,698	754,986
78	754,986	37,749	0	118,974	55,364	63,611	729,125
79	729,125	36,456	0	122,662	57,080	65,582	699,999
80	699,999	35,000	0	126,465	58,849	67,616	667,383
81	667,383	33,369	0	130,385	60,674	69,712	631,041
82	631,041	31,552	0	134,427	62,555	71,873	590,720
83	590,720	29,536	0	138,594	64,494	74,101	546,155
84	546,155	27,308	0	142,891	66,493	76,398	497,065
85	497,065	24,853	0	147,321	68,554	78,766	443,152
86	443,152	22,158	0	151,887	70,680	81,208	384,102
87	384,102	19,205	0	156,596	72,871	83,725	319,582
88	319,582	15,979	0	161,450	75,130	86,321	249,240
89	249,240	12,462	0	166,455	77,459	88,997	172,705
90	172,705	8,635	0	171,616	79,860	91,756	89,585

Third, what if you are lucky enough to outlive the plan's payouts? Suppose you live to be 95, not 90? Under the trajectory in Chart 2, you may well have depleted your retirement savings account by then, leaving a big deficit in your budget for each additional year you live.

The implication is that you may wish to take out a kind of insurance policy to hedge against such surprises. The simplest way to do this is to buy a fixed annuity, which is sometimes described as a "do-it-yourself pension."

Here as well, we treat the pros and cons of various types of annuities later, in Chapter IX. The point for now is simply that a well-designed and carefully researched fixed annuity can provide a solution to the problem of outliving your nest egg.

Worksheet

Part A

TOTAL PERSONAL SAVINGS NEEDED FOR RETIREMENT

A   Estimated Gross Preretirement Income.. _____

B   Replacement Rate (Table 3, Column 2).. _____

C   Equivalent Retirement Income (line A × line B).. _____

D   Estimated Annual Income from Social Security (Monthly Benefit × 12)*....... _____

E   Estimated Annual Pension Income (if any) .... _____

F   Estimated Annual Income needed from Savings (line C – line D – line E)....... _____

G   Estimated Unadjusted Total Personal Savings needed (line F × .25)**.......... _____

* From the "Personal Earnings and Benefit Estimate Statement," available from the Social Security Administration.

** As explained in the text, a multiple of 25 corresponds to an annual inflation-adjusted withdrawal of four percent.

20

Part B

ESTIMATED REQUIRED ANNUAL SAVINGS*

(a) Age Saving Begins	(b) Unadjusted Savings from line G	(c) Savings Factor from Table 4	(d) Annual Savings [line G × (c)]	(e) Monthly Savings
____	_____	_____	_____	_____
____	_____	_____	_____	_____
____	_____	_____	_____	_____
____	_____	_____	_____	_____
____	_____	_____	_____	_____
____	_____	_____	_____	_____
____	_____	_____	_____	_____
____	_____	_____	_____	_____

Note: We have provided space here for you to enter a number of estimates based on different assumptions respecting your income, the age when you begin saving, inflation rates, etc.

III.
COVERING LIFE'S CONTINGENCIES

THE future is not ours to see. Unexpected contingencies can derail even the most carefully crafted retirement savings plan. These might include:

- Divorce,

- the premature death or disability of a breadwinner,

- job loss,

- the loss of health insurance before 65,

- the need to care for aging parents,

- the mounting expense of a college education.

How common are such financial curve balls? They can hit you at any time, of course, but they are especially burdensome for those in later mid-life, doing everything they can to save for retirement. Among this group, it turns out, disruptions—unexpected or worse-than-expected financial stresses—are the rule, not the exception.

One recent analysis of people between 51 and 61 showed that 69 percent experienced at least one major "life shock" during the 10-year interval. The authors found that medical setbacks were most common among the life-events studied, but that nearly 20 percent of the people studied were laid off, and nearly 10 percent lost a spouse to death or divorce. (See Chart 3.) By this reading, only three out of 10 people go through their fifties without facing a setback likely to derail retirement saving. Many will experience more than one setback.[1]

Accordingly, this chapter considers some ways to plan for the unexpected, to help you balance retirement goals and competing claims. In light of major changes in 2006 in the law concerning long-term care financing, much of the chapter deals with the sometimes difficult and expensive problem of caring for aging parents.

Life Insurance, Disability Insurance

You may have coverage for *life insurance* through your employer. If not, and if your and your family still face major expenses such as college tuition, a mortgage, or other outstanding debts, you may need to get it on

---

[1] "How Secure Are Retirement Nest Eggs?" by R. Johnson, G. Mermin, and C. Uccello, April 2006, Center for Retirement Research, Boston College.

your own. The key consideration is the capacity of your surviving spouse or other dependents to handle debts, bills, and similar obligations. If you have no financial dependents, you do not need life insurance.

Very often, the amount of life insurance provided by employers is not nearly enough to cover such obligations, so you may need to obtain additional insurance on your own. One advantage of doing this is that, in contrast to employer-sponsored insurance, you will not lose this coverage in the event you lose or leave your job. It may cost more than corresponding coverage obtained through an employer. You may be required to get a medical examination as proof of insurability. But if your circumstances warrant it, life insurance can protect you or your family in essential ways.

As to what kind of policy to get, term life insurance is usually the best bet. It is the cheapest way to obtain a given amount of coverage. A term policy provides coverage for a specific amount of time, from one year to, say, 25 years. A benefit is paid if the insured dies during the period. If he does not, the policy expires with no value. There is no investment component to a term life policy (in contrast to whole life or other "cash value" policies, which are more expensive).

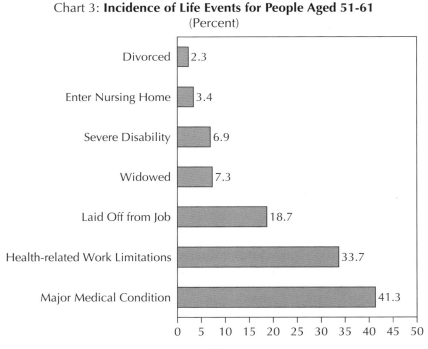

Chart 3: **Incidence of Life Events for People Aged 51-61**
(Percent)

You can compare quotes on term policies from different insurance companies by consulting an insurance broker or going on-line. However, many websites are little more than marketing tools operated by insurance companies and brokers. According to the Consumer Federation of America (CFA), a non-profit consumer education organization, the best sites to obtain on-line quotes for term life are www.InsWeb.com, www.quotesmith.com, and www.term4sale.com. For more information on CFA's evaluation of on-line quotes, visit www.consumerfed.org.

Disability insurance covers the chance that an accident or protracted illness reduces the covered person's income and may also trigger continuing medical costs. While not as clear-cut a requirement for most people as life insurance, it may make sense for "one-paycheck" families, or single people, depending on circumstances. That way, if the breadwinner's income from employment ends, disability payments help fill the gap.

This is a good place to note the difference between disability insurance, which is mainly to provide for loss of income, and *long-term-care* insurance. Though sometimes confused, the two cover quite different contingencies.

As the name implies, long-term-care insurance provides mainly for nursing-home expenses. These days, it may also cover some at-home coverage as well. Either way, it refers to patients (and the vast majority are elderly) who need special care. As such, it does not provide payments to make up for lost income, but only to cover health care and nursing-home costs. To qualify for benefits, the insured must be unable to perform basic activities of daily living such as dressing, bathing, eating, and getting in and out of bed.

Disability insurance, on the other hand, pays benefits if you are unable to do your current job or its equivalent. You may not be "disabled," in the everyday sense of the word, but simply not able physically to do the specific tasks (like loading a moving van, for example) that had been part of your job. Some employers offer long-term or short-term disability coverage as a work benefit; some employers even pay all or part of the premium.

Health Insurance: Loss of a Group Plan before 65

Many people retire, either voluntarily or through corporate "downsizing," well before Medicare benefits begin at age 65. Others would like to retire early. They all must face the question of how to obtain health insurance. Many employers used to provide health insurance to their early retirees, covering them until Medicare began, but fewer offer this benefit nowadays. At the same time, employers are shifting the burden of paying for retiree health insurance premiums to their former employees. According to the Kaiser Family Foundation, only about one-third of companies with 200 or more workers now offer retirees some form of health benefits, down from 66 percent in 1988. A growing roster of companies including Sears, General Motors, and several airlines, have recently cut retiree benefits, or are considering doing so. Others have established ceilings on how much they will pay for retirees' health insurance.

If you are one of the many people whose employer does not offer continued health benefits after retirement, *you should line up alternative coverage before you leave*. You can try to obtain individual coverage, although you may need to go through medical underwriting. Premiums will vary widely and depend on a number of factors, including your age, health, the policy's deductible, and your state's regulations. If you have health issues, even minor ones, you might be turned down for coverage or the premiums may be unaffordable. If you have always relied on your employer to provide a policy and perhaps pay all or most of the premium, be prepared for a shock: individual health insurance policies can be hard to find, the benefits may be less comprehensive than your group policy, and they are often very expensive.

During your search, you should be aware of two protections for those seeking health care coverage who have been separated from the workforce. The Consolidated Omnibus Budget Reconciliation Act (COBRA) gives workers and their families who would otherwise lose their health benefits the right to choose to continue their group coverage under their employer's plan for limited periods of time under certain circumstances, such as voluntary or involuntary job loss, reduction in the hours worked, transition between jobs, death, divorce, and other life events. However, while employers must allow you to keep your coverage, they do not have to pay your premium. *Qualified individuals may be required to pay the entire premium for coverage*. For family coverage, this can easily be $1,000 a month.

Employers are generally only required to offer COBRA coverage for 18 months (and small employers may be entirely exempt). After coverage ends, you are eligible for an individual policy under the Health Insurance Portability and Accountability Act (HIPAA) of 1996. Under this law, people who have had continuous coverage are "guaranteed" the right to individual coverage. "Continuous coverage" means covered in a group plan or by COBRA with gaps in coverage of no more than 63 days. What is not specified in the law is the price you will have to pay for coverage. It may be high, particularly if your health qualifies you only for coverage in a state's "high-risk" pool. (People can fall into this category even if they have seemingly minor health problems.)

In general, HIPAA provides rights and protections for participants and beneficiaries in group health plans. It limits coverage exclusions for pre-existing conditions. It prohibits discrimination against employees and dependents based on their health status. It also specifies rights you have to coverage when you change jobs, leaving one group-health plan behind and entering a new one. The website for the Department of Labor (www.dol.gov) offers more information on your health insurance rights when you leave your employer.

Some would-be early retirees look at their limited health insurance options and decide not to retire early after all. Others work part-time after "retirement," either for their former employer or at another job, in order to receive health care benefits. Although such jobs may not pay as much as your former full-time position, they may be worth considering as a way to obtain group insurance.

If you are still several years from retirement, you might consider setting up a separate savings account for health care costs. If your employer offers one, a health savings account (HSA) can also be a good way to prepare for future medical expenses. Contributions to these accounts are federally tax-deductible and earnings accumulate tax-free, as long as they are used to pay for qualified medical and retiree health expenses. However, they must be used in conjunction with a high-deductible health insurance plan. You can obtain more information from employers who offer these plans, or from a booklet titled, "All About HSAs," available at the Treasure Department's website at www.treasury.gov.

After you reach age 65 and become eligible for Medicare, you will need to consider ways to fill the gaps in that program's coverage.[2]

Caring for Elderly Parents

The mounting costs of ongoing care for a loved one in deteriorating health present a financial challenge that often falls on family members who are trying to save for their own retirement.

The cost of such care depends in part on the setting in which it is provided. Home care, assisted-living communities, and nursing homes are three options. Nursing homes are generally the costliest choice. On the other hand, of course, staying home can be more expensive if the person needs round-the-clock care due to declining physical or mental health.[3]

According to the MetLife Mature Market Institute, the average cost for a private room in a nursing home in 2005 was $200 a day, or $73,000 per year. As with housing prices, such cost variations tend to display large contrasts

---

[2] See our book *How to Cover the Gaps in Medicare: Health Insurance and Long-Term Care Options for the Retired* for guidance in this area.
[3] See our book *How to Choose Retirement Housing* for a timely and more extensive treatment of the issues discussed in this section.

between urban areas on either coast, compared with inland, rural locales. In the New York metropolitan area, for example, the costs can average $125,000 or more. While short-term skilled nursing-home care is covered by Medicare, long-term or custodial care is *not*. However, such care is covered by Medicaid (the government health-care program for the poor), assuming the patient's income and assets are low enough to qualify.

While ongoing care for the elderly can be costly, there are ways that families can help mitigate these expenses. Some, such as "Medicaid planning" or long-term-care insurance, can be put in place years before someone enters a nursing home or other long-term care setting.

Others, such as a reverse mortgage, may provide a quick solution to an immediate and pressing financial need. However, reverse mortgages on homes owned by seniors work *only as long as the elderly person lives in the home*. If and when they must leave home, they are obliged to sell the home or repay the mortgage. Moreover, these loans have high fees.

In any case, legislation signed into law in February 2006 sharply restricts the availability of Medicaid to pay for nursing-home care. (Indeed, some lawyers have termed it "the nursing-home bankruptcy act.") By the same token, the new rules encourage the use of long-term-care insurance, reverse mortgages, and at-home care.

Medicare—Many people believe this will help cover the long-term elder care costs of themselves or their parents, but Medicare does *not* pay for long-term care services or long-term assisted-living costs. Instead, it is designed to cover the cost of short-term "skilled" or nursing care provided in a nursing home or contracted through a home health care agency. It only pays for the first 20 days, and in part for an additional 80 days, of care in a skilled nursing facility following a hospital stay of at least three days. It also covers the cost of part-time nursing or therapy services for people living at home, if prescribed by a physician.

Medicaid—The government program that does pay for much of the expenses recorded nationwide for long-term care is Medicaid, which in theory is intended only for poor people, *i.e.*, those with very low incomes and very limited assets. Not surprisingly, figuring out how to qualify as "poor" in the face of nursing-home expenses running above $70,000 a year has become something of an art form—and given rise to a specialization called "elder-care law" among attorneys.

Medicaid pays for about half of all stays in nursing homes. Private long-term-care insurance covers less than 10 percent, Medicare pays a small portion, and the remainder—nearly 30 percent—is paid by patients and families out-of-pocket.

To be eligible for Medicaid assistance, patients in nursing homes must have limited assets *and* must contribute all of their income toward the cost of care.

Assets counted in determining Medicaid eligibility include funds held in checking and savings accounts, stocks, bonds, retirement funds from which withdrawals can be made, and real estate. *Exempt* assets have included a home, a car, and funds designated for burial expenses. (We will say more about the home as an exempt asset shortly.) Technically, covered assets must be reduced to $2,000 for a single person to qualify for Medicaid financing of nursing-home care. At that point, any income, such as Social Security or a pension, will go to Medicaid as compensation.

In practice, states have wide latitude in setting rules for how assets will be counted for the purpose of determining Medicaid eligibility. For example, individual states may provide incentives for families to take out long-term-care insurance, in exchange for the right to hold on to additional assets to go into an estate.

2006: Congress Tightens Up on "Medicaid Planning"—Although Medicaid was designed as a safety net for people with low incomes and few assets, many middle-class people (and some wealthy ones) have long engaged in what is known as Medicaid planning. For many, this involved *converting eligible assets into exempt assets* through measures such as paying off all outstanding debt (including a home mortgage), investing in home repairs, or buying a car. Any remaining liquid assets (remaining, that is, after all the other money has been spent) could be "annuitized." An annuity could be purchased that yielded income that was fully or partially exempt from the regulations—and in the event of the death of a spouse, could even go to the children.

For couples with liquid assets over $350,000 or so, this sort of "spending down" was not always sufficient to convert assets to exempt-category status. These people had several options, including asset transfers through gifts and special "Medicaid trusts."

Over the years Congress periodically has tightened the rules in hopes of thwarting some of these spend-down efforts and thereby forcing wealthier people to pay for more of their care. Some years ago, Congress established periods of ineligibility for Medicaid financing for those who transferred assets. Such "penalty periods" usually lasted for 36 months, although certain kinds of asset transfer triggered longer periods. Under the old rules, the penalty period (to repeat, a period of ineligibility for Medicaid financing), began with the date of the last asset-transfer.

When were such asset transfers of interest to Medicaid officials? The relevant interval came to be known as the "look-back period." If such asset transfers occurred less than three years before someone applied for Medicaid financing of nursing-home care, there would be a penalty period. In other words, state Medicaid officials generally kept track of transfers made within 36 months before the Medicaid application (60 months when the transfer was made through certain kinds of trusts).

Under the old rules, even those who had not planned ahead could still protect about half their savings by giving them away, typically to their heirs. Before applying for Medicaid, a prospective applicant could transfer half of his assets and begin the penalty period. He could then use the other half of his resources to pay for care while waiting it out. After the penalty period was over, he could apply for Medicaid coverage.

Now the rules have changed. It appears that Congress concluded that the old system placed too much of the tab for nursing-home costs on government—meaning, in the end, taxpayers.

Debate has long centered on the question of whether middle-class and wealthy individuals or couples should be allowed to impoverish themselves to qualify for a benefit intended for those of limited means. Rather than a legitimate means of preserving the estates of hard-working families, critics labeled the practice of Medicaid planning as an unfair and deceptive sheltering of assets. This, apparently, was the view that shaped the 2006 law.

Table 6: **Key Changes in the 2006 Medicaid Law**

1. *Planned monthly gifts* (formerly permitted up to $5,700) are now prohibited as a way to "spend down" assets.

2. *The "look-back" period* to keep track of asset transfers has been extended for families from three years to five years.

3. *The penalty period* now begins when one applies for Medicaid, rather than when the last asset transfer took place.

4. Any *balance for an annuity* a well spouse has initiated must go to the state to pay Medicaid costs for the ill spouse when the well spouse dies (not to the children).

5. Medicaid financing is no longer available to an individual having *home equity* above a cap ranging from $500,000 to $750,000 (varying by state). Anyone with equity above the threshold will have to reduce it, by selling their home or borrowing against it, before Medicaid will pay for nursing home or other long-term-care services.

6. The new home-equity cap rule does not apply *if the applicant's spouse remains* in the home, regardless of its value, but would apply if the spouse died.

As Table 6 shows, now the rules governing gifts and asset transfers are more severe (or even "punitive," in the view of some elder-care lawyers). Planned monthly gifts, which had been tolerated, are now prohibited. The start of the penalty period (formerly measured from the date of the last asset-transfer) now comes on the date one *applies* for Medicaid—when, after all, the applicant's assets have already been depleted. Further, the look-back period for families has increased from three to five years. In addition, any balance of an annuity that a healthy spouse may have purchased can no longer be passed on to the children when the healthy spouse dies, but must instead go to pay Medicaid for the sick spouse. Such changes appear to make planned asset-transfers far less feasible.

The net effect is to shift financing responsibility from the government to families. As that shift asserts itself over the next year as states redesign their individual Medicaid programs to meet the new federal rules, a variety of responses are likely to emerge. Medicaid planning is not likely to disappear, but those who wish to engage in it should never attempt asset conversion without first consulting an attorney and accountant who specialize in this complex area. Also, as already noted, there will be new and greater roles for (1) long-term-care insurance, (2) reverse mortgages, and (3) at-home care.

Long-Term-Care Insurance—This pays for care in a variety of settings—in a nursing home, at home, or in assisted living—for people who cannot perform basic activities of daily living without help, such as eating, dressing, toileting, and getting in and out of bed. Years ago, consumer groups viewed long-term-care insurance as an oversold, overpriced product riddled with exclusions. In the last decade, however, many of the more objectionable features of these policies have been eliminated. Still, long-term-care insurance is a complex product requiring thorough evaluation. It is not always an optimal solution.[4]

The general view has long been that long-term-care insurance is neither for the very rich nor for the poor, but for certain families in between. Families with considerable wealth can "self-insure," meaning pay for care out-of-pocket. Low-income families can apply for and receive Medicaid. Those with assets worth $250,000 to $500,000 (above and beyond the value of their homes) are the likeliest candidates, financially speaking, for long-term-care insurance.

Nevertheless, this perspective may be outdated. The new Medicaid rules seem intended to encourage middle-income families generally to buy long-

---

[4]Here as well, see our book *How to Cover the Gaps in Medicare: Health Insurance and Long-Term Care Options for the Retired* for a fuller discussion of this issue.

term-care insurance. In particular, a practice formerly restricted to only a few states has now (as of February 2006) been opened to all. Now, states can allow families to shield more of their assets as exempt from being taken to pay for a nursing home or long-term care, provided the families take out long-term-care policies. Considering the stringency of the new provisions on asset sheltering, this could prove a powerful inducement.

Nor are the benefits of a long-term-care policy confined to nursing-home costs. It may help family members keep an elder at home as long as possible. By paying for many services provided at home (or, later perhaps, at an assisted-living facility), long-term-care insurance can help postpone the transfer to a nursing home as long as possible.

On the other hand, pricing and benefits can be difficult to gauge, or to compare. Sales people may encourage couples to purchase coverage when they are in their forties or fifties to capture a lower premium. In general, this is not cost-effective.

For most people it makes sense to wait until their sixties to decide on a long-term-care plan. Waiting longer gets expensive: A single 75-year-old in good health would currently pay about $10,000 to $12,000 a year for a typical policy. On the other hand, buying when you are younger is less expensive—for the same coverage, a healthy 48-year old would pay about $2,500 a year—but there is no guarantee that you will ever need the policy. You might pay tens of thousands of dollars over the years and never make a claim.

Another consideration is the stiff underwriting standards that people must meet in order to buy a policy. When you (or your parents) apply for a policy, the insurance company will evaluate your physical and mental condition. The older you are, the more thorough the evaluation. If they detect any indication that you are likely to be a candidate for long-term care down the road—your memory is failing, you are unsteady on your feet, you have a history of health problems that could someday require chronic care—they will not sell you a policy. In essence, if your (or your parents) wait until you "need" a policy, you will not be able to get one.

Another issue is how long the benefits will continue to be paid once the insured goes into a nursing home. For example, one policy we have seen costs a reasonable $1,100 a year—but the fine print shows that this premium covers only six months (or $45,000, whichever is less) of nursing-home care. To be sure, half the people who enter a nursing home are there for less than six months (partly because some of them go there to die). But for cases of stroke, dementia, or the comatose, six months of coverage might be only a stop-gap.

In short, there are other variables besides premiums. Beyond cost, and whether you are in the market for long-term-care insurance for your parents or yourself, you should also consider the following features:

- *Stability of the insurer.* In recent years, a number of companies have exited the long-term-care insurance market. A presence in the market for at least 12 to 14 years and a high rating by A.M. Best (a company that rates the financial strength of insurers) can provide some degree of assurance that the insurer is financially stable and will be around when the benefits come due.

- *The policy's coverage and facility options.* Different policies cover different types of care and levels of service. For example, some cover respite care, services in assisted living facilities, or hospice care. Others do not.

- *The amount of the daily benefit.* Most policies pay a set dollar amount per day, week, or month and usually limit the total benefit they pay over the life of the policy. If you can pay some expenses yourself, you can purchase less coverage and save on premiums.

- *Benefit triggers.* When does a person become eligible for long-term-care benefits? The degree of impairment that triggers benefits varies widely. So do the standards for judging impairment. Also of interest are waiting periods that must pass before benefits begin to be paid.

For detailed comparisons of specific policies, check the periodic evaluations in *Consumer Reports* magazine, on-line at consumerreports.org. Their most recent survey appeared in the November 2003 issue; it is available on the website.

Reverse Mortgages — Homeowners over 62 can draw on a reverse mortgage to help pay for their care or other expenses in retirement. Under this arrangement, the lender advances money to an older person in exchange for a future claim on the home. You can use the proceeds for anything, and some people use the money to refurbish their homes so they can continue to live there, while others use it to pay for the cost of personal care or other assistance.

The homeowner can also use the proceeds to pay premiums for a private long-term-care insurance policy. However, if you cannot afford to buy such a policy without borrowing against your home, it is questionable whether you should buy it or whether you even need it. Also, the optimal time to take out a reverse mortgage is not necessarily the optimal time to buy a long-term care policy. Reverse mortgages are a better deal for older homeowners (in their seventies and later). But if you wait until then to buy a long-term care policy, you might not be medically eligible and the premiums will be very high.

Under the most common type of reverse mortgage, called a Home Equity Conversion Mortgage (HECM), the lender advances money to a homeowner in a series of fixed monthly payments, a line of credit, or a combination of the two. The borrower need not repay the loan as long as he or she remains in the home. The lender collects the balance of the loan when the borrower moves out, sells the home, or dies.

The amount of the loan generally depends on a borrower's age and the home's value. The older you are, and the more valuable your house, the more cash you can get.

HECM closing costs, including an up-front mortgage insurance premium, can be financed through the loan. The amount needed to pay off an existing mortgage, to cover future loan service charges, and to pay for any home repairs that might be needed to qualify, can also be financed through the loan. But doing so reduces the money available to the homeowner. In some cases, these charges significantly reduce the available cash. In others, the combination of up-front charges and compounding *interest on the loan* can bring the final loan balance well above the amount the borrower received.

The total amount that must be repaid can never exceed the value of the home at the time of repayment. Nonetheless, these loans are costlier than conventional mortgages.

Consider this cautionary example from Georgetown University researchers: A 70-year-old borrower with home equity of $80,000 might opt for a loan paying him about $380 a month over a life expectancy of 15 years. At the end of that period, he would have received a total of $68,392 and would owe $103,523 — $1.51 for every dollar received. It is an even worse deal if the proceeds are used to pay for long-term-care insurance premiums. The combination of high insurance costs (which may never actually pay benefits, depending on whether you make a claim) and high borrowing costs brings the average value of actual long-term-care benefits down to just 36 cents for every dollar of forfeited equity.

Such calculations of course depend on the specific numbers and interest rates used. No matter what the particulars, however, two essential caveats should be noted.

One is that whatever money is borrowed and used through a reverse mortgage reduces the size of the homeowners' estate. To that extent, the instrument should not be used lightly, even under the best of terms.

Second, the high up-front costs make a reverse mortgage attractive only for people who intend to remain in their homes for years to come. For someone about to move out of their home within a year or two, the high initial costs have the effect of sharply raising the annual interest costs of the loan.

Aging in Place

Still, and in light of the 2006 legislation, it has now become more desirable to use a reverse mortgage to "elder-fit" your home and to remain there as long as possible. More generally, and reverse mortgages aside, many people want to do whatever it takes to help people remain in their own homes as they age. Of course, people have always really wanted "to stay home" if at all possible. Similarly, many people faced with the issue of caring for aging parents would doubtless like to help them stay at home as long as possible. The question is, how can you make that option more realistic and safe?

Surveys show that two main concerns seniors have about their living quarters are (1) physical safety, including safety from crimes, and (2) being able to live self-sufficiently in a living space that is "senior friendly." Given the first, what can people to do approximate the second? What can someone living in, say, a three-story house, where the desired living space is separated by stairs, do?

One answer, increasingly, is an elevator. Changes in technology have brought the costs of an effective home elevator down to the $25,000-$35,000 range.

This example is mentioned because, while at first blush extreme, it provides perspective on the kinds of changes that can be made as people grow older, aging in place. Is $30,000 a lot of money? Not compared to the cost of a year in a nursing home. And certainly not when averaged over a number of years.

By the same token, there are many other changes you can make to your (or your parents') house to make it more suitable for aging bodies and minds—or at least, less threatening. Elevators, stair gliders, ramps, lighting, security systems, plumbing arrangements—these and many other fixtures and add-ons can help make a house safer, more secure, and more comfortable for people beyond 65.

At the same time, all that is the easy part of the assignment. The hard part is finding skilled, reasonable, and above all trustworthy people to serve as at-home caregivers—and coming up with the money to pay for such blue-ribbon services. But more often now it can be done, as support organizations are springing up to make it easier. As with assisted-living facilities also, whatever postpones a nursing home is probably worth the effort.

College or Retirement?

As they are saving for a retirement that may be less than a decade away, many parents face the unexpectedly high cost of college. Even though they may have been saving for years they may still be unprepared for the $150,000 cost of four years at an elite private university. Adding the cost of graduate school makes the price tag for an education even more overwhelming.

The question many parents face is whether to reduce or even eliminate their own retirement plan contributions and redirect the savings to pay for college costs. Unless they have accumulated a substantial nest egg that is already adequate to meet their financial needs after retirement, the answer is a resounding "no." Given today's high cost of education, it is not unreasonable for parents to require children to foot at least some of the cost of their college education through scholarships, employment income, loans, and other means if they cannot manage to squeeze those costs into their own budget. Alternatively, they might seek less expensive alternatives such as a public university. Children have many years to repay student loans, while the time frame that parents require to save adequately for retirement may be much shorter.

Getting Your Estate in Order

As you organize your retirement finances and plan for unexpected contingencies, this may be a good time to draft or update your estate plan if you have not already done so. *The Estate Plan Book*, written by attorney William S. Moore and published by AIER, provides guidance on estate planning. Of course, you should consult your own attorney or other advisors for expert assistance tailored to your unique circumstances—not only for estate planning but for the other topics we have surveyed in this chapter.

IV.

SOCIAL SECURITY

FOR all the debate surrounding how to handle what many see as a coming crisis in Social Security, no changes have been made yet to the program. Eventually it is likely that changes will have to be made, that either taxes will have to be raised or benefits trimmed. But Congress may well put off doing anything until the long-predicted financial problems actually materialize.

Social Security's financing problem is mainly demographic. Under the current "pay as you go" system, contributions collected from workers in the form of payroll taxes are not invested for future retirement, but are immediately paid out as benefits to current retirees. The payments retirees receive are financed, in other words, by payroll taxes on current workers. The more current workers per retiree, then, the easier the financing burden.

The problem is that this ratio of current workers to retirees has been falling and will continue to do so. The Social Security Administration projects that the number of retirees will grow rapidly starting in 2008, when the members of the post-World War II baby boom generation begin to reach early retirement age. The number of retirees is projected to double in less than 30 years.

Today, there are roughly three workers for each retired person. But because people are living longer and birth rates are low, the ratio of workers paying Social Security taxes to people collecting benefits is expected to fall from 3.3 today to 2.1 by 2032. Even before that—by 2017, according to the latest official projections—tax revenues will fall below program costs. If no changes are made to the system, by 2040 the Social Security Trust Funds are projected to be empty. Of course, it is unlikely that nothing will be done. The question is what, and when.

The debate surrounding how to handle the shortfall in future years came to the forefront in 2005, when President Bush floated the idea of private savings accounts. The proposal proved too controversial and has since been tabled by the Bush Administration.

What was the proposal, and why did it spark so much opposition? Under such a system, younger workers would divert payroll taxes from Social Security to fund private accounts, which they would later tap to support themselves in retirement. The idea stands in sharp contrast to the pay-as-you-go approach, under which today's taxes are immediately paid out to current retirees.

Supporters of Social Security personal savings accounts said that by investing in stocks and bonds, workers could receive higher benefits, and perhaps leave a nest egg to their heirs. Critics countered that personal retirement accounts mean higher risks for workers, and that if investments were not doing well when a worker is ready to retire, plans would have to be changed. They also said personal accounts could be expensive to administer. Another issue was how to pay for them—how to divert payroll taxes into private accounts and have enough tax money left to continue paying traditional Social Security benefits for the current generation of retirees and workers nearing retirement.

Now the Bush proposals are no longer in play. Other options under consideration include :

1) Reducing benefits or slowing their future growth. One way of doing this would be to increase the retirement age for full Social Security benefits. Critics of the proposal to further raise the retirement age say most Americans now choose to retire early, and that it would be hard for some people to work past the current retirement age because of their health or because their jobs are just too demanding. Another way to do it would be to change the formula that is used to calculate benefits. In this way, for example, benefits for higher-income retirees might be scaled back.

2) Raising Social Security taxes. The current combined (employer plus employee) payroll tax rate is now 12.4 percent. Critics argue that payroll taxes are already very high, and point out that eventually Social Security taxes would have to be raised substantially to pay for all benefits owed.

3) Having the government invest Social Security reserves in stocks and bonds. That way higher potential returns could be earned but financial risks shared. Critics say the government should not invest in private companies, because the government could end up being the largest stockholder in a company.

4) Having the government borrow more. The government already borrows to pay for some of its activities and it could borrow more. However, such borrowing can have negative effects on the economy, and the interest would have to be paid by future generations of taxpayers.

It is hard to avoid the conclusion that effective Social Security "reform" will combine a mixture of measures, combining lower benefits, higher taxes, and delayed retirement. For today's younger workers, meaning roughly speaking those under 45, the outlook is highly uncertain. Perhaps the only safe assumption about their Social Security benefits is that the rules are subject to change between now and the time they retire. Their benefits are likely to be less generous than today's, their payroll taxes raised, and the age at which they are entitled to collect full benefits increased.

On the other hand, those facing retirement within the next few years can probably plan on a stable set of rules and procedures governing Social Security benefits and eligibility. For them, the question is how the system works now. Accordingly, we turn now to questions of current benefit levels.

Benefits under the Current System

The Old Age, Survivors and Disability Insurance (OASDI) program provides monthly benefits to retirees, dependents, widows, spouses, divorced spouses, and disabled workers. According to the Social Security Administration, at the end of 2005, 48 million people were receiving benefits: 33 million retired workers and their dependents, 7 million survivors of deceased workers, and 8 million disabled workers and their dependents. The focus in this chapter is on retirees and survivors, who numbered 40 million at the end of 2005.

Provided they are "fully insured," both male and female workers become entitled to "early" or reduced retirement benefits at age 62. In general, 40 quarters (10 years) of participation in the program (generally, paying payroll taxes) are required for an individual to be fully insured.

Your full or normal retirement age depends on when you were born. Beginning in the year 2000, the full retirement age began to increase gradu-

Redefining "Normal"	
Year of Birth	Normal Retirement Age (to collect full Social Security benefits)
Before 1938	65
1938	65 and 2 months
1939	65 and 4 months
1940	65 and 6 months
1941	65 and 8 months
1942	65 and 10 months
1943-1954	66
1955	66 and 2 months
1956	66 and 4 months
1957	66 and 6 months
1958	66 and 8 months
1959	66 and 10 months
1960 and After	67

ally and will become age 67 in the year 2022. (Early retirement benefits are still available at age 62, but at a 25 percent discount from "full" benefits, as explained shortly.)

As the box on page 39 shows, the change affects those born after 1938. People born between 1943 and 1954 reach full retirement age at 66. For those born after 1954, the full retirement age rises by 2-month increments until it tops out at 67 for people born in 1960 or later.

Social Security does not pay benefits automatically as soon as you become eligible. To begin collecting benefits, you must file an application. You should plan to do so about two months in advance, and have a copy of your birth certificate. The process may take longer and require more paperwork for the self-employed. For information on filing, or any other Social Security question, you can contact the Social Security Administration at the toll-free number 1-800-772-1213, or visit the administration's web site at www.ssa.gov.

For those who qualify for benefits as spouses, widows, divorced spouses, and dependents, benefits may not be available until either the beneficiary or the worker reaches a certain age, and there are various other conditions that must be met. If you fall into one of these categories, regardless of your income it may pay to check with your local Social Security office about possible eligibility for benefits. A surprising number of eligible people do not collect benefits simply because they did not realize they were eligible and never thought to apply for them.

Estimating Your Benefits

The amount of the benefit payable to a fully insured individual depends on his or her average taxable earnings during the years of covered employment. Because of various changes in the law over the years and the need to index for price inflation, calculation of benefits is complicated. A simple presentation of typical results is not feasible.

In practice, most people receive a "Benefit Estimate Statement" in the mail from the Social Security Administration each year a few months before their birthday, with updated projections of their eventual retirement benefits.

If for some reason you do not receive this annual update, you can request a free estimate of your benefits from the Social Security Administration. You must complete a "Request for Earnings and Benefit Estimate Statement" (Form SSA-7004) available from your local office or through a toll-free number (1-800-772-1213). You can also use one of the benefit calculators available at the web site, www.ssa.gov.

Of course, the further away your retirement is, the more likely the official estimate will change as your earnings record changes. If you are close to retirement, however, the benefit estimator is very useful for planning.

The Benefit Estimate Statement also includes year-by-year totals of earnings subject to the payroll tax, and the amount of tax paid. It is worthwhile to keep your own earnings records (or failing that, your federal income-tax copies) and to check them against this statement every few years. If the official records are in error, you may receive smaller benefits than what you should receive. Such errors do occur. At one time the Social Security Administration estimated that nearly 19 million earnings reports had incorrect names or Social Security numbers, and thus those earnings could not be properly credited.

As a guideline, the *maximum* monthly Social Security benefit for a person retiring in 2006 at the normal retirement age is $2,053. (Once again, "the normal retirement age," as listed in the box, is the age required to collect "full" Social Security benefits, currently 65 years and 8 months for those born in 1941.) In practice, few people receive this maximum. The *average* monthly benefit actually paid out to currently retired workers was just over $1,000 at the end of 2005.

Under current law, benefits are adjusted for price inflation each year, starting with the year you reach age 62. (The benefit is adjusted whether you are collecting it or not.) This automatic adjustment is an exceptional feature of Social Security: hardly any private pensions provide for this, generally because they cannot afford it. The adjustment for 2006, for example, raised 2005 benefits across the board by 4.1 percent.

Family Retirement Benefits

When you become eligible for Social Security retirement benefits, your spouse may also be eligible for benefits based on your earnings record. *You must begin collecting your benefit before your spouse can begin collecting a benefit based on your record.* For spouses who have reached the full retirement age, the spousal benefit is equal to 50 percent of your "primary insurance amount" (an amount, based on Social Security's benefit formula, which serves at the basis for calculating your own Social Security benefit). Alternatively, your spouse can apply for this benefit any time after reaching age 62, but the benefit will be permanently reduced. For example, if a wife elects to collect benefits at age 62, her benefit would be reduced by 25 percent. This works out to a benefit equally to 37.5 percent of her husband's full retirement benefit.

The amount of the reduction depends on the spouse's full retirement age. If it is 66 (the age for those born between 1943 and 1954), a 62-year-old spouse can get 35 percent of the worker's unreduced benefit. If full retirement age is 67, the spouse can get 32.5 percent of the worker's normal benefit.

In today's two-earner families, many spouses will find themselves eligible to collect benefits based on their own earnings record, in addition to being eligible for a spousal benefit. When that happens, Social Security will not pay both benefits in full — but will pay the higher amount.

Families may be eligible to collect an even larger retirement benefit. A spouse caring for a child under 16 is eligible to collect spousal benefits at any age, with no reduction made for the spouse's age. Dependent children who are under age 18 (19, if in high school) or permanently disabled also are eligible to collect benefits equal to 50 percent of the retiree's full benefit. Again, none of these benefits are payable until the retiree's benefits begin. Moreover, conditions for eligibility vary, so check with your local Social Security office.) There is a maximum family benefit, which, like all Social Security benefits, is adjusted each year for price inflation.

Survivor Benefits

Survivor benefits are available to spouses at virtually any age if they have young children, and to the younger children as well, providing the deceased qualified as "insured." Survivors of a deceased worker should always investigate their eligibility; never assume you do not qualify because of income or other circumstances.

Of particular interest to retirement planners, as early as age 60 a surviving spouse can claim a benefit based on the deceased's Social Security. However, a benefit equal to the deceased's full retirement benefit is available only if the spouse waits until full retirement age to claim it. Benefits claimed between age 60 and full retirement age are reduced permanently, on a sliding scale. For a 62-year old widow (or widower) of someone whose normal retirement age was 65, the benefit is 82.5 percent of the full benefit; for a 60-year old it is 71.5 percent.

As with spousal retirement benefits, if you become eligible to collect your own retirement benefit in addition to a survivor's benefit, Social Security will pay the larger amount, not both.

Early Retirement

You can receive full retirement benefits only upon reaching the full retirement age. However, you may collect early retirement benefits any time after your 62nd birthday. At present more than half the people eligible for benefits sign up at 62 — even though they receive only 75 percent of what they could get by waiting a few years until full retirement age. To be clear: these benefits are *permanently* reduced from their full retirement level.

There are advantages and disadvantages to taking early retirement benefits, some of which will be obvious only to the individual. One issue in the decision is that Medicare coverage does not begin until age 65, even if you are receiving Social Security benefits at an earlier age. So if you actually stop working when you elect to begin collecting early benefits (you are not required to do so), you must arrange for adequate health insurance, perhaps through your former employer, until then.

For some it may well make sense to claim benefits early. Although your monthly benefits will be smaller, you will probably receive them for a longer time. The total amount you receive over your lifetime if you retire early may well be as much or even more than you would get if you waited.

The reduction for early retirement varies depending on whether you were born before 1943 or were born later, as follows:

If you were born before 1943...	**If you were born in 1943-1954...**
20% reduction at age 62	25% reduction at age 62
13 1/3% reduction at age 63	20% reduction at age 63
6 2/3% reduction at age 64	13 1/3% reduction at age 64
(Your full-benefit age is 65)	6 2/3% reduction at age 65
	(Your full-benefit age is 66)

For workers who were born after 1954, the reduction for early retirement will be higher yet. Depending on the year you were born, the reduction if you claim benefits between ages 62 and 67 will be as high as 30 percent.

An example may clarify the financial trade-off involved. Suppose you were born in 1944 and turned 62 in 2006. Your full retirement benefit, say $1,000 a month, would come at age 66, in 2010. If you retire early at age 62, your monthly benefit will be permanently reduced by 25 percent, or $250, to $750. Total "extra" benefits received by retiring 48 months before full retirement age would be $36,000 (48 times $750). Dividing the boost you would get by instead waiting until age 66, $250 per month, into $36,000 results in 144 months, or 12 years. This is how long it would take for the larger benefit you would get by waiting until 66 to outweigh the extra benefits you could receive by starting to collect at 62. So, if you do wait, you would come out ahead only if you live to be older than 78 (66 + 12). In this sense, 78 can be termed your "break-even" age.

However, as another consideration, the financial advantage of early retirement decreases somewhat if a spousal benefit is involved. The reason? The spousal benefit, which is 50 percent of the worker's benefit, decreases to less than 50 percent if the working spouse takes early retirement.

Late Retirement

Not only do your benefits increase if you wait to your full retirement age to collect. They also increase if you then keep waiting, and *they go up every year you wait until you reach 70*. The amount of the increase varies from six to eight percent, depending on when you were born, as follows:

Year of birth	Yearly increase rate
1935-1936	6%
1937-1938	6.5%
1939-1940	7%
1941-1942	7.5%
1943-or later	8%

For persons who turned 65 in 2006, the increase from waiting is 7.5 percent per year. For those born in 1943 or later, hence turning 66 in 2009 or later, the increase will be eight percent a year. This increase applies regardless of whether you are still reporting earnings. It affects only your own benefit, not spousal or family benefits. After age 70 there are no more automatic increases.

Longevity and the Retirement Decision — for Men and for Women

The healthier you are in your 60s, the more it may make sense to wait to claim initial benefits. As already noted, health enters into the calculation because the longer you live, the more likely it is you will live beyond the "break-even" age for total lifetime benefits.

From that perspective, it has been suggested that married men should wait until full benefits are available, but married women should enroll as early as possible. According to Professor Alicia Munnell of Boston College, whereas half of people becoming eligible at 62 now choose early retirement benefits, the early sign-up generally makes the best sense for *married women and single men*. The reasons differ, but the stark logic is the same.

For married women, their low benefits from enrolling early are only temporary. When their husbands die (probably well ahead of them, statistically speaking), the new widows have the option of taking the higher payment, hers or his.

As for single women in their 60s, they can expect, on average, to live well beyond 80. By waiting and taking higher benefits, they can expect to live long enough to make the postponement worthwhile.

What about men as a group? Here also, differences in longevity come into play. For both men and women, the choice of when to enroll depends on how long they expect to live. In fact, the Social Security website has an odd tool called a "break-even calculator" that shows how long you have to live to reap the advantage of postponing enrollment until you receive full benefits. (Recall that in our earlier example, we came up with a break-even age of 78.)

What does the break-even calculator have to do with married men? Only that, statistically speaking, married men tend to live longer than single men. To that extent, single men might be better off enrolling early, while married men should give more thought to waiting. These statistics are merely averages across the population, of course, and their usefulness for making individual decisions is limited.

Sometimes It's All There Is…

What have we left out of the discussion of timing? The main omission is probably the role of economic necessity. Even if everyone had a crystal ball as to their longevity, financial circumstances vary widely, and some people would simply find an early benefit check too hard to pass up.

In 2004, for example, over a third of elderly recipients had virtually no other income. According to the Social Security Administration, "benefits comprise 90 to 100 percent of total income for one-third of the elderly beneficiaries; and for almost two-thirds…it is their major income source (50-100 percent of their income)." The specific shares are shown here in Chart 4. Putting it differently, only a little over a third of retirees derived more than half of their income from other sources.

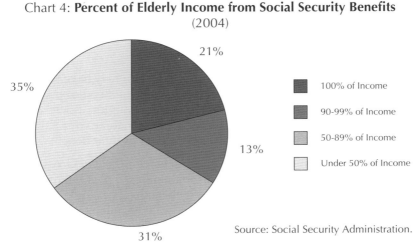

Chart 4: **Percent of Elderly Income from Social Security Benefits**
(2004)

- 100% of Income
- 90-99% of Income
- 50-89% of Income
- Under 50% of Income

Source: Social Security Administration.

The implication is that many people cannot afford to wait when they turn 62. Some of them, of course, will continue to derive income from employment, whether full- or part-time. If so, they will encounter limits on how much they can earn from employment, while still retaining their allotted Social Security benefits.

The Earnings Test

To receive benefits, retirees must meet the requirements of a Social Security earnings test. But note that "earnings" in this context do not include income from savings, investments, pensions, insurance or annuities.

Instead, the earnings cap refers to the amount persons below full retirement age may earn *from employment* and still receive benefits. If earnings exceed the limit, benefits will be reduced.

If you are under the full retirement age when you start getting your Social Security payments, $1 in benefits will be deducted for each $2 you earn above the annual limit. For 2006, that limit is $12,480. In the calendar year you attain full retirement age, $1 in benefits will be deducted for each $3 you earn above a higher annual limit up to the month of full retirement age. For 2006, that limit is $33,240.

The good news is that upon reaching the "normal" retirement age with full benefits, *you can earn an unlimited amount from employment* without any direct reduction in benefits. The "Senior Citizens' Freedom To Work Act of 2000" eliminated the Social Security annual earnings test in and after the month in which a person attains full retirement age.

On the other hand, if you are still working after your full retirement age, your earnings from employment, coupled with your Social Security benefits and other income, could push your total income up to a level that could make some of your Social Security benefits taxable.

Taxes on Benefits

If your retirement income is sufficiently high you may have to pay Federal income tax on some of your Social Security benefits. For people with "provisional income" below $25,000 ($32,000 for couples), Social Security benefits are tax-free. However, retirees with such income over a threshold amount may owe income tax on up to 85 percent of their benefits.

"Provisional income" in this instance includes Adjusted Gross Income (earnings, pensions, dividends, and taxable interest), plus interest on tax-exempt bonds, *plus* half of Social Security benefits. For single persons, 50 percent of such provisional income over $25,000, plus an additional 35 percent of any excess over $34,000, is taxable. For married persons filing joint returns, the income thresholds are $32,000 and $44,000. The effect for high-income retirees can be to subject all but 15 percent of their Social Security benefits to the income tax.

Given that only those with income above a certain level pay income tax on their Social Security benefits, these benefits are, in effect, subject to what amounts to an undeclared means test. Of more importance to future retirees, *these tax thresholds are not indexed for price inflation.* Today about two-thirds of retirees have incomes below the threshold, according to the Social Security Administration. But unless the law is changed, that fraction will grow over time. In a process similar to the "bracket creep" that pushed people into higher tax brackets in the 1970s, future inflation will push more retirees over the income limit for tax-free Social Security benefits.

Other tax issues can come into play concerning the treatment of benefits when you (1) continue to have earnings from employment and (2) as a result also have "provisional income" above the thresholds just listed. These interactions can be fairly complicated and are not easily summarized here. For more information on tax liabilities during retirement, talk to your tax advisor or ask the IRS for a free copy of its Publication 554, *Tax Benefits for Older Americans* and Publication 915, *Social Security Benefits and Equivalent Railroad Retirement Benefits.*

Will Social Security Be Enough?

While Social Security is a keystone in most people's retirement and it provides substantial benefits, they are unlikely to be enough to live on. The higher your pre-retirement income, the more likely you are to need other source of income to keep up your standard of living. For a couple reaching full retirement age in 2006, with one working spouse earning the maximum taxable earnings of $94,200, Social Security benefits might replace only about 35 percent of those earnings.

If your earnings were significantly lower, Social Security might replace a much higher portion. That indeed is how the program was designed to work. As the Social Security Administration puts it, "The level of pre-retirement (career-average) earnings replaced by Social Security benefits for a worker retiring at full retirement age varies because *the benefit formula is progressive. It is weighted in favor of workers who have lower earnings* since they have less opportunity to save and invest during their working years."

By the same token, people with higher average earnings over their careers need to take advantage of their greater opportunities to save and invest for retirement. Even though the Social Security benefit will give them an inflation-indexed annuity, it is unlikely to be adequate as a sole source of retirement income.

Moreover, in the long run—when today's younger workers retire—benefits could well be less generous than they are today, given the financial and demographic pressures on the program. For these reasons it is important to provide for supplementary retirement income through pensions, earnings, income-producing assets, and personal savings.

Accordingly, the next four chapters consider the various ways you can supplement Social Security benefits with traditional pensions, 401(k)-type accounts, IRAs, and other forms of investment.

V.

THE (DISAPPEARING) TRADITIONAL PENSION

W HEN President Bush signed the Pension Protection Act of 2006, he said that it introduced "the most comprehensive reforms to America's pension system in over 30 years." He neglected to mention that this pension system, which has provided generous benefits to millions of today's retirees, is rapidly becoming a thing of the past.

By pensions, we mean *defined-benefit* pensions. These are the traditional gold-watch plans, where employees work their 30 or 40 years for the same company, then retire with a gold-watch ceremony and a fixed-dollar monthly benefit for as long as they live.

This sort of arrangement is rapidly approaching extinction, at least among private-sector employees. Employers find the plans too costly to fund, and the costs are also unpredictable. The amount they must set aside each year to fund them can change markedly whenever, as is usually the situation, investment returns, price inflation, and wage rates differ from the actuaries' assumptions. Employers increasingly prefer to pass the burden of invest-ment risk to workers by offering them 401(k)s instead.

Traditional Plans, 401(k)-Type Accounts, and IRAs

The defined-benefit or gold-watch approach flourished in the decades after World War II, then peaked in the 1980s. As Chart 5 shows, since 1980

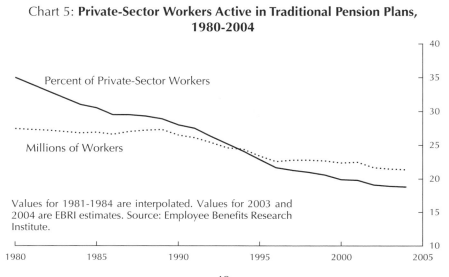

Chart 5: **Private-Sector Workers Active in Traditional Pension Plans, 1980-2004**

Percent of Private-Sector Workers

Millions of Workers

Values for 1981-1984 are interpolated. Values for 2003 and 2004 are EBRI estimates. Source: Employee Benefits Research Institute.

the share of the private-sector workforce enrolled in traditional pension plans has fallen from over a third (35 percent) to less than a fifth (about 19 percent in 2004).

Today defined-benefit plans are most often offered by (1) governments (federal, state, and local) and (2) older, larger, and unionized companies. Few if any new plans are of this type. (Appendix A links the decline in defined-benefit plans in the private sector to a sequence of federal pension laws dating back to 1974.)

In their place, employers have increasingly shifted to or initiated plans that place more responsibility on the employee. This second employer-based version is the *defined-contribution* plan, as symbolized by the 401(k) account. (The name derives from the statute in the law that authorized the approach).

Under 401(k)-type plans the employer—or the employee, or both—may make contributions based on percentages of the employee's salary, and the proceeds go into separate retirement accounts for each employee. The amount available at retirement depends on the total contributions made and on the rate of return earned over time on the investments in the account.

In terms of total savings, the 401(k)-type plans have now overtaken the gold-watch pension. In 2004, assets in traditional defined-benefit pension plans totaled just under $2 trillion. As Chart 6 shows, this amount lagged behind 401(k)-type defined-contribution plans, which had reached $2.5 trillion.

In any case, both of these employer-based plans trail a third form of retirement saving, *individual* retirement accounts, or IRAs. As the name

Chart 6: **Retirement Plan Assets in Trillions of Dollars, 2004**

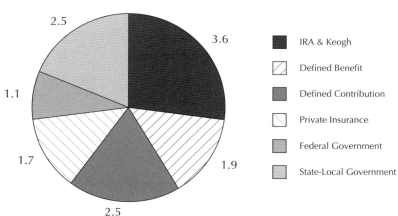

Source: Employment Benefits Research Institute.

50

implies, IRAs are initiated and maintained by individuals, independently of their employment ties. At the end of 2004 IRAs held $3.6 trillion. One reason this sum is so large is that IRAs serve as a "parking place" for tax-sheltered accounts when people leave a job and cash out a 401(k)-type account as a lump sum.

The sector in which traditional defined-benefit plans still dominate other arrangements is government. Chart 6 also shows that between the federal and the state-local tiers, the funds in government accounts add up to another $3.6 trillion. Most of that is attributable to traditional pension plans. The regulatory framework (or, better said, lack of regulation, especially for states and localities) makes public-sector pension plans a breed apart. (For more on this issue, and on the question of inadequate funding of public-sector pensions, see Appendix B.)

Still, even in the private sector, and despite the continuing shift by companies to other approaches, *for many people traditional pensions are and will continue to be a vital source of retirement income*. It has been said that pensions are to higher-income retirees what Social Security is to lower-income retirees: the keystone. Accordingly, this chapter describes the mechanics and tactics for managing defined-benefit or traditional pensions.

Funding (and "Underfunding") Defined-Benefit Plans

Employers are legally liable for the specified dollar benefits owed to employees, and must fund defined-benefit plans with whatever amount of contributions is needed to meet this benefit liability. An employer's benefit liability includes not only benefits currently owed to retirees, but an estimate of the total value of benefits to be paid in the future to current and past employees.

The value of future benefits depends on many factors that can only be conjectured, such as future wage levels, job turnover, mortality rates, life expectancy, inflation rates, and interest rates. Economic and actuarial assumptions are used to estimate this liability, and if the value of the pension fund equals this estimated liability, the pension plan is said to be "fully funded." If the liability is greater than the pension fund, the plan is "underfunded."

Pension laws require that a minimum level of funding be maintained. Since the value of a pension fund, and the actuarial estimate of the benefit liability, can vary dramatically from year to year, pension funds can rather suddenly become "underfunded." This does not necessarily mean they are in financial distress. This measure of a plan's financial health considers only *whether a plan's fund is sufficient to pay off immediately all benefits that would be owed if the plan were suddenly to shut down*. In actual situations, the liability does not fall due all at once but is amortized over many years,

51

and an "underfunded" plan therefore may not be financially untenable over the long run.

In some instances, however, underfunding can be a serious financial problem, eventually leading to the termination of a defined-benefit plan. The liabilities of qualified defined-benefit plans are insured, however, by a government agency, the Pension Benefit Guaranty Corporation (PBGC). In the event a financially unsound plan terminates, employee benefits (up to a legal maximum) are guaranteed by this agency.

Oddly enough, another factor in the decline of defined-benefit pensions has been "overfunding." If a plan contains funds in excess of the estimated benefit liability, an employer may terminate the plan, pay off owed benefits (in cash or by purchasing annuities for the beneficiaries), and retain the excess funds for other uses. As Appendix A describes, that scenario became increasingly common in the 1980s, in part because it was the only way companies could reclaim the excess in funding.

Loss of Benefit Value Due to Price Inflation

From the employee's point of view, one of the main reasons to prefer a 401(k)-type account is that over time, investments in such accounts are more likely to keep up with price inflation. By contrast, the traditional pension's typical fixed-dollar monthly payment is especially susceptible to inflation's ravages.

Few private plans provide for full "inflation indexing" of benefits for retirees. Typically, benefits are only partially indexed, or they are increased on an irregular basis, when the rate of price inflation is deemed especially high by fund managers and "excess" funds are available to pay for increased benefits. Many plans provide for no cost-of-living increases at all.

The resulting losses can be substantial. For example, a benefit of $1,000 would lose a third of its purchasing power after ten years of "moderate" four percent annual price inflation. With life expectancies higher and early retirement more common, the real value of a fixed-dollar benefit now steadily erodes over a longer period of time than in previous generations.

That is why you should check with your employer for a benefit estimate that you can use in your retirement planning. In particular, ask if there are any provisions for adjusting your benefit for inflation. If not, at least you have a realistic understanding of the problem and can take steps to deal with it through other forms of saving.

Vesting and Other Plan Provisions

Under a defined-benefit plan, you have little control over the way benefits are calculated or your employer's management of the pension fund. You can influence the amount of your benefit, however, by taking full advantage of *vesting* — the process by which you acquire, over a number of years, a legal claim to your benefits.

Before retiring (or switching jobs prior to retirement) review the vesting rules of your pension plan. You may find, for example, that by staying with the firm another year or even another month, you could earn a much larger benefit.

Many workers have at best a vague understanding of what they must do to ensure they will receive the maximum benefit due to them. A misunderstanding of the specific provisions of a plan can result in an employee receiving a much smaller benefit than he or she expects.

One obstacle is confusing terminology. An employee who is "covered" by or "participating" in a plan is not necessarily entitled to receive benefits. *Only a "vested" employee has a non-forfeitable claim to promised benefits, regardless of whether the employee remains with the company until retirement.* An employee may be "partially vested," having a claim to only a percentage of earned benefits. A "fully vested" employee has a legal claim to all earned benefits.

To earn a vested claim to employer contributions, an employee must work for the company for a minimum number of years specified in the plan. Federal law currently requires that a participating employee be fully vested after five years of service *or* 20 percent vested after three years, with another 20 percent each year thereafter (resulting in full vesting after seven years). To be credited with a year of vested service, an employee generally must work 1,000 hours a year (with a 40-hour workweek, this takes about six months). If you do not work the minimum required hours, you may receive no credit toward vested service.

Vesting requirements become particularly important when you are planning to leave your job or retire, the more so when a plan provides for *cliff vesting*. Cliff vesting provides an employee with full vesting after a certain number of years, and zero vesting before that time. (Many plans currently provide for five-year cliff vesting: employees have no vested rights until they have five years of credited service, after which they are 100 percent vested.)

If an employee participating in, say, a five-year cliff vesting plan leaves the job after four years, or even after four years and 999 hours, all benefits are forfeited, and the employee receives nothing except the return of any employee contributions, plus interest. If the plan had instead provided for partial vesting of an additional 20 percent every year, then the opportunity to gain an additional 20 percent share of earned benefits would have been lost.

Because vesting requirements can make such a difference in determining your pension benefit, you should carefully consider them, if possible, in timing your decision to retire or leave a job.

Timing and Coordination

Oddly, a year's credit for vesting purposes is not necessarily the same as a year's credit toward benefits. A plan may require more than 1,000 hours of work for an employee to be credited with an additional year of service used in figuring the benefit or contribution earned by the employee. In the previous example of a 5-year cliff vesting plan, after 1,000 hours in the fifth year of service the employee would be 100 percent vested, but, depending on the plan's requirements, might not be credited with a fifth year of service for purposes of calculating earned pension benefits until after, say, 1,500 hours of service.

There may be other provisions in a plan that can be easily overlooked or misinterpreted, but may be of great importance in determining the amount of your pension and when you can collect it.

For example, some plans are "integrated" with Social Security, and may either reduce the earned pension benefit by the retiree's Social Security benefit, or reduce the employer's defined contribution to a pension fund by the Social Security tax paid by the employer. An employee unaware of this integration will receive a much smaller pension than anticipated.

As another example, a plan might offer an employee the option of receiving the value of a pension in one lump-sum payment if the employee leaves the job before retiring, but only if the employee makes a written request for this *before* actually ending his or her service. If such a request is not made, the benefits may not be available until retirement.

The wisest course is to avoid making any assumptions about your pension plan, and to read a copy of the plan thoroughly to understand its provisions, especially before retiring or leaving a company.

Job Mobility and Portability of Benefits

Since plans are designed to reward career employees the most generously, workers who change jobs frequently may end up with disproportionately smaller pension benefits. As mentioned above, non-vested benefits earned with one company are lost upon switching to another company, and with each new job a new vesting period must be satisfied.

Non-vested benefits are thus said to lack "portability." Yet even a worker who earns vested benefits in a succession of jobs is likely to end up with a smaller pension than one who, with the same career earnings history, remains with one company until retirement.

To repeat, it is a good idea to review the provisions of a plan and consider the possible loss of benefits when considering a job change and the timing of a decision to leave a job.

Early Retirement

There is no longer a mandatory retirement age for most jobs, but many plans define the "normal retirement age" as 65. Retirement benefits may be available prior to this under an early retirement provision, by which benefits may be collected before age 65 but usually only after a certain number of years of service. No employer is required to offer this option, and the age limit for early retirement varies with every plan.

The amount of the benefit is usually permanently reduced by an actuarially based percentage to account for the additional years of benefits the employer expects to pay. The specific reduction, if any, will be described in the written plan. Other retirement benefits, such as health, medical, dental, and life insurance may be modified for workers choosing early retirement. It is essential to provide for medical insurance until age 65, because Medicare coverage does not begin until then, even if a retiree is collecting early retirement Social Security benefits.

Spousal Benefits

Many pensions payable as annuities, including defined-benefit pensions, must provide spousal survivor benefits. Pension law requires that annuity benefits be paid in the form of a *joint-and-survivor annuity* unless the retiring employee specifically chooses a higher-paying single-life annuity. Under the joint-and-survivor annuity option, benefits continue to be paid to the spouse after the retiree's death, but the monthly benefit is reduced over the retiree's life and more so over the surviving spouse's life. (The surviving spouse's annuity must be at least half of the annuity payable to the participant during the couple's expected remaining lifetime together.)

By contrast, the *single-life annuity* provides for an unreduced benefit, paid only until the retiree's death, with the survivor receiving nothing afterwards. Prior to the passage of the Retirement Equity Act of 1984 (REA), the worker could choose the single-life annuity without informing the spouse, and consequently a widow or widower could be left with no benefits at all, without her or his prior consent.

Under the 1984 law, the retiring married employee may still waive the *automatically provided* joint-and-survivor annuity option, in favor of a single-life annuity, but such a waiver now requires the written and notarized consent of the spouse. Couples may wish to consider waiving the option if, for example, the retiree seems likely to outlive the spouse, or if the retiree has sufficient life insurance to provide for the spouse. (Conversely, having chosen the joint-and-survivor option, no life insurance may be necessary.)

The REA also provides for a *pre-retirement survivor annuity* to be provided automatically to the spouse of a worker who dies before retirement. This option may be waived only with the written and notarized approval of the spouse. According to the law, benefits will be paid to a vested worker's spouse at the plan's earliest retirement age whether or not the participant had retired or was eligible for early retirement at the time of death. If the pre-retirement option is chosen (or, more properly, not waived) the worker's benefit will usually be permanently reduced by an actuarially based percentage.

Pension law also requires spousal consent if an employee elects the option, where available, of receiving his or her benefit in the form of a lump-sum distribution rather than an annuity.

Finally, the REA specifies that pension benefits can be divided in the event of divorce, and may be treated as alimony or property (most are awarded as part of a property settlement). Settlements vary widely, as there is no minimum award required. Divorced spouses are entitled to collect awarded benefits as soon as the plan participant reaches the earliest retirement date provided under the plan, regardless of whether the participant has actually retired. The method of payment must be one allowed by the plan; for example, a lump-sum payment can be awarded only if a plan provides such an option. In some cases, nonvested benefits may also be awarded, and a plan participant who never actually becomes vested may be responsible for funding the award by other means.

Lump-Sum Distribution or Fixed-Dollar Annuity?

Before you leave a job or retire, ask whether you have the option of taking your pension benefit in a lump-sum distribution rather than as a fixed-dollar annuity benefit. Employers are not obligated to offer this option, and in any case it may be offered only to employees who have participated in a plan for at least five years. If it is available, review carefully the financial advantages and tax consequences of taking a lump-sum distribution.

Each choice has its advantages and disadvantages. A fixed-dollar benefit provides the assurance that you will receive a specific amount of money over your post-retirement lifetime, or perhaps over the remaining lifetimes of you and your spouse. However, unless the benefit includes cost of living increases—a feature found in few plans outside of those for civil service employees—your monthly income will be eroded by the impact of price inflation.

On the other hand, if you invest a lump sum payment and achieve good returns through investing you could simulate a pension through regular withdrawals and keep pace with inflation, or better. But you won't have the assurance of receiving a given amount each month.

To some extent, the decision of whether to take a fixed-dollar benefit or a lump sum depends on your outside resources. If you have other assets and income, such as an IRA, you could opt for the regular monthly check from the pension plan and use your investments for growth, or for discretionary expenses. You could also roll the lump sum into an IRA, then use part of it to fund an annuity that will provide regular monthly income, and part for investments.

Finally, as you approach retirement age you should notify all past employers of the date of your retirement and your address. Even if you are not going to stop working, notify them when you reach the normal retirement age. This will ensure that you receive all benefits to which you are entitled

Tax Treatment of Pension Benefits

The tax treatment of retirement savings, benefits, and cash withdrawals depends on the type of plan, the form of payment (annuity or lump sum), the amount received, and the beneficiary's age. For traditional, defined-benefit pensions, the picture is relatively simple. If the pension is wholly based on employer contributions, proceeds from an annuity are subject to income tax. Indeed, income taxes on employee pension benefits usually are withheld automatically unless you request otherwise.

If, on the other hand, you receive your pension as a lump-sum payout, other tax considerations come into play. These are described in the next chapter,

VI.

401(K)-TYPE RETIREMENT PLANS

THE other major type of employer-based retirement program is the *defined-contribution* plan, such as a 401(k) account. What is "defined" in this case is not a monthly pension benefit, but the amount to be contributed into an investment account by employees and employers.

As noted in the last chapter, many companies began to move from traditional to defined-contribution plans during the 1980s and 1990s. The shift has accelerated in recent years, as even blue-chip companies like Coca-Cola, IBM, and Verizon have terminated traditional fixed-benefit plans, while sweetening the terms of 401(k) accounts. By late 2005 an estimated 47 million private-sector employees were participants in 401(k) accounts, over twice the number in defined-benefit pension plans.

The Pension Protection Act of 2006 includes new regulations that are intended to make 401(k) plans more effective in helping workers to save for retirement. Judging by the new law, Congress apparently believed that as traditional pension plans have faded, too few employees were taking full advantage of 401(k) and related plans. Under the 2006 law, newly hired employees will be automatically enrolled in a company's 401(k) plan. In the past, they had to "opt in," but now they will have to "opt out." In other words, they will have to make an explicit decision *not* to participate in a monthly savings plan. The new law (along with recent court decisions) may also encourage more employers to offer "cash-balance plans," a hybrid of traditional pensions and 401(k)s (these are discussed in more detail later). These plans seek to combine the flexibility of 401(k)-type accounts with the reliability of defined-benefit ("gold-watch") pension plans.

Defined-Contribution Vehicles

The various types of defined-contribution plans include:

- 403(b)s, the precedent, for non-profit organizations (legislated in 1958);

- 401(k)s, tax-sheltered contribution plans offered by companies (1978);

- 457 plans, like 401(k)s, for state and local government workers (1978);

- Federal Thrift Savings Plans, tax-deferred saving for federal workers (1986);

- Roth 401(k), a 401(k) paid for with after-tax dollars, beginning in

59

2006; and

- Cash-balance plans, hybrids of defined-benefit and 401(k)-type approaches.

Except for the last entry, a hybrid, these variations on the basic model are linked by one big outcome. The retirement benefit in a defined-contribution plan is not directly tied to the employee's salary or years of service. Instead it depends on the market value of the account at the time of retirement. *The employer assumes no liability for guaranteeing a specific benefit* and no obligation beyond making any promised contributions during an employee's years of service.

In 2005 nearly three-fourths of the employees of medium-sized and large businesses (and one-third of those in small businesses) participated in a 401(k)-type plan, according to the Congressional Budget Office.

When employers choose (at their discretion) to match part or all of employee contributions, the result is called a "savings and thrift plan." In 2005, about 70 percent of employees with 401(k) accounts received matching contributions from employers. The match formulas ranged as a rule from 25 to 100 percent, with 50 percent as the most common ratio. An employee contributing six percent of her salary in such a plan could have it matched by three percent from the employer, for a total of nine percent of her salary.

The 2006 limit for how much an employee may shelter from taxes in a 401(k) account is $15,000 (or, for workers 50 or over, $20,000). But the actual limit, as a percentage of salary, can be smaller, at the discretion of the employer. (The average limit in 2002 was 16.5 percent, according to the Congressional Budget Office.)

Your own contributions made to such a plan are immediately fully vested. This makes the accounts far more portable in the event of a job change. However, you may have to be "vested" before you are entitled to your employer's contributions. The vesting schedules allowed by the law are the same as those for defined-benefit plans. With some plans, you will be vested immediately, but with others, you may not be fully vested for as long as five years.

As a legal matter, "under-funding" of defined-contribution plans is not a problem. That is, federal pension laws intended to ensure adequate financing and actuarial design of defined-benefit pensions do not apply to defined-contribution plans. Why? *By definition they are always fully funded.* There is no need to insure that funds are sufficient to pay promised benefits; if the value of the fund is low, the value of the benefit also will be relatively low. Moreover, the administrative costs for companies of estimating future benefits also are eliminated.

Defined-contribution plans still must comply with various tax laws, however, to be considered "qualified plans," *i.e.*, eligible for favorable tax treatment of contributions. They must comply with participation and coverage rules that apply to all private pension plans, as well as various laws concerning limits on contributions and proper fiduciary management of funds.

Can there be "under-funding" in any other sense? Yes, to the extent that you do not take full advantage of the power of 401(k)-type plans to provide for your retirement. It is said that one-fifth to one-third of employees who could take part in 401(k)-type plans neglect to do so, even in some cases when employer matching is available. Among Americans who have retirement accounts, most have less than $40,000 in them. Even employees on the eve of retirement typically have less than $100,000 in them. Under-funding in this distinct sense overlaps with the larger problem that, according to virtually all available data, Americans are not saving much. Many have doubtless benefited from soaring home prices in recent years, but that is a thin reed for longer-term financial security.

Tax Advantages

To see why it is usually in your interest to enroll in a 401(k) or similar plan, first consider the powerful financial benefits of sheltering contributions from current taxes. It helps to work through an example or two of how tax-sheltered salary-reduction plans take advantage of compound growth over time.

As noted above, the salary-reduction option or "elective deferral" feature of a 401(k)-type plan allows an employee to choose to have part of his or her salary go to a retirement fund rather than have it paid as salary today. The tax advantages of this are two-fold. First, earnings that you contribute are not counted in your taxable income (although they are subject to Social Security tax). Second, the investment returns earned in your account are also tax-deferred.

In addition, employers may match your contribution, in full or in part. As a result, you can earn a much higher return on your 401(k)-type investment than you could in comparable investments outside of the plan.

To illustrate, suppose you have the option of contributing to such a plan in which your employer contributes one dollar for every two dollars of salary you elect to contribute. If you contribute $2,000 ($167 per month), you immediately reduce your taxable income by $2,000. If your marginal tax rate is 28 percent, you would save $560 in Federal income taxes.

In addition, your employer makes a matching $1,000 contribution — giving you an instant "return" of 50 percent. If the total $3,000 investment earns a tax-free return of seven percent, in 20 years it will grow to $11,600 — a cumulative return of 480 percent on your original investment. Of course, eventually you must pay income taxes on this amount. Even after paying 28 percent in taxes, however, the account would be worth $8,350.

On the other hand, suppose you choose not to contribute to your pension plan. The $2,000 in earnings is taxed as income, leaving you with $1,440 to invest (assuming your tax rate is 28 percent). If you put this money in a conventional savings account where interest earnings are taxed as income, the annual seven percent return would be reduced to a 5.04 percent after-tax return. After 20 years your investment would grow to $3,850, less than half the after-tax value of the tax-favored investment.

Beginning in 2006, some employers are offering another type of plan called a *Roth 401(k)*. With this new plan, employees make contributions on an *after-tax* basis. In other words, they pay taxes up-front on whatever wages they contribute to the plan. However, unlike a traditional 401(k), withdrawals are not subject to taxes—as long as the participant is at least 59½ and the money has been held in the account for at least five years.

In other words, Roth 401(k)'s are to the original variety as Roth IRAs are to traditional IRAs. In the Roth versions of each, you pay this year's taxes on income, and using the after-tax dollars that remain, you contribute to the 401(k) or IRA. After that, any earnings on the account are tax-sheltered, as are the withdrawals you make at retirement age.

In 2006, for Roth 401(k)s as for traditional ones, the contribution limit is $15,000—or, under the catch-up provision, $20,000 for those age 50 or older.

Even if Your Employer Contributes Nothing…

Matching contributions from your employer make such plans an all but unbeatable investment. In essence, if your employer offers to contribute to your plan, deciding not to participate is akin to failing to accept a raise or a bonus.

But even if your employer does not match your contribution, the favorable tax treatment of your own investment and of the earnings on it still make it more attractive than most other methods of saving.

In the above example, if your tax-deductible salary deferral of $2,000 (with nothing extra from your employer) were invested tax-free at seven percent for 20 years, it would increase to roughly $7,700. In other words, it would be worth twice what could be earned if your wages were initially taxed at 28 percent and the remainder were invested in a taxable account. The difference is smaller over a shorter time, but it still favors the retirement account.

This is a good place to emphasize again how helpful it is to start putting aside 401(k) savings early on. For instance, if you were to contribute $1,000 of salary into a 401(k) plan each year from age 20 through age 29 *and nothing more after that*, and if you left the funds invested at a return of eight percent, at age 60 you would have over $157,000. By comparison, if you waited *until* age 30 to begin contributing to your retirement account, and then deferred $1,000 of salary *every year after that* until you reached age 60, you would have only $123,000. In other words, 10 years of saving early on would outgrow 30 years of saving later on. The earlier you start, the more you gain.

Comparing 401(k)-Type Plans to Traditional Pensions

From the employee's viewpoint, then, there are several advantages to defined-contribution plans. This is especially true where companies match employee contributions, whether dollar for dollar or at some lower ratio.

While a participant in such a plan does not have the security of a fixed-dollar benefit, he or she gains the opportunity to realize an enlarged benefit if the fund earns a high return. And as we pointed out in the last chapter, fixed-dollar benefits provide only an illusion of "security" of purchasing power in the face of inflation.

The issues for traditional pensions as to vesting and job changes are not as significant with 401(k)-type accounts, since any contributions you make yourself are immediately vested. Defined-contribution plans provide more pension portability. That is, they allow you to take the account with you when you leave a company, rather than wait until retirement to receive a benefit. The funds in your account can then be reinvested to earn a return until you retire.

Finally, such plans often allow for greater employee management of funds. Within limits, most plans allow employees to switch funds from one investment account to another, thereby allowing them to balance risk and return according to their own preference rather than the employer's.

In theory, then, if your employer offers a 401(k)-type plan, your course is clear. First, obtain a copy of the plan from your employer. To maximize your benefits, you should take a salary-reduction rate that would take full advantage of any employer matching formulas. If your employer matches at 50 percent up to a limit of $6,000, try to put that much into the account. Having tax-sheltered the resulting $9,000, you should then diversify the holdings in your account to the extent permitted by the plan.

In practice, however, a disadvantage for employees has turned out to be that a 401(k)-type plan requires *decisions* they are not always comfortable making. First and foremost is the decision to join or not to join a plan. Many have not taken advantage of the opportunity, at times even when employers offered to match worker contributions. For those who do sign on, many participants tend to choose low-return but "safe" investments, like money market funds, which over the long haul leave them without much growth. Others put all their retirement eggs in one basket, loading up on their company's stock.

More generally, there is growing evidence that the difficulty of decision-making in the face of seemingly complex choices is one reason for the failure of many employees to participate in their plans or, once they sign up, to regularly review their investments or follow basic guidelines for investing, such as choosing an appropriately diversified mix of assets. In short, many workers do not have the time, expertise, or inclination to manage their money in ways that professional money managers would consider sensible or rational.

Concerns about this helped shape the 2006 pension-law overhaul, in ways that reduce the number of explicit decisions employees have to make about their accounts. The new law also opens the door for employers to provide more investment education for employees.

"Automating" 401(k)-Type Plans: The 2006 Pension Law

Other motives played a part in the design of the Pension Protection Act of 2006. Without trying to say which mattered most, we can list a few of the major influences on the end result:

1. Businesses saw traditional defined-benefit pensions as expensive and unwieldy.

2. The Pension Benefit Guaranty Corporation appeared to face a funding crisis.

3. The rising prominence of 401(k)-type plans exposed defects that needed fixing.

4. Social Security was unlikely to fill the growing gap in retirement finances left by vanishing defined-benefit pensions.

5. There was ample evidence that many Americans have not saved much toward their retirement.

6. Mutual funds and financial advisors wanted more business.

In other words, the traditional three pillars of retirement financing — pensions, Social Security, and personal saving — had come to look increasingly shaky as the basis for most Americans' retirement strategy. Concerning the vexing problem of companies like United Airlines declaring bankruptcy and turning their pension commitments over to the government (via the Pension Benefit Guaranty Corporation), Appendix A surveys that issue and touches upon measures in the 2006 law to strengthen the PBGC's funding.

Here we focus on the new rules that are most important for current workers. At the same time, it should be understood that *nothing in the new law changes the benefits or terms for people already in retirement.*

The main changes affecting companies and their employees take place as of 2008. (Note, however, that nothing stops companies from adopting the approaches advanced in the new law before then, if they like. Fidelity Investments, for example, is re-tooling its management of 401(k) accounts for its client companies to help them ramp up early.) Some of the effects and outcomes will depend on the specifics and interpretations of supporting regulations (which, at this writing, are yet to be spelled out).

Pending such refinements, here are some key rule-changes affecting employees:

- New employees at companies offering 401(k)-type plans will be automatically enrolled in company plans, with the right to "opt out" if they so choose.

- Moreover, companies are encouraged to increase the share of employee wages and salaries going into the accounts, year-by-year, *e.g.*, when raises are given.

- Companies are encouraged (but not required) to match employee savings.

- Companies must offer three forms of assets to invest in, beyond company stock.

- The "default investments" for employee accounts will be mutual funds (stocks), not money-market funds or other low-risk, low-return investments.

- Accounts will be "managed" either by a "certified" computer model or by financial advisors, including representatives of mutual-fund companies.

- Companies will be encouraged to offer "safest available annuities" to retiring employees, converting lump-sums into a pension-like stream of income.

As you might guess, the 900-plus pages of the Pension Protection Act contained other items as well. Among them are these provisions of interest to specific income groups or demographic niches: (1) The tax credit for low-income savers that was scheduled to expire in 2006 has been made permanent. It allows for a tax credit up to $2,000 for retirement saving (in IRAs, 401(k)s and other plans) for some low- and middle-income workers. (2) Now people other than a surviving spouse can also inherit the amount in a 401(k) account, placing the proceeds into an "inherited IRA," and minimizing the tax on withdrawals by stretching them out according to the heir's life-expectancy. (3) The tax exemption for withdrawals from college savings accounts, previously set to expire in 2010, has been made permanent. This makes such "529 plans" more appealing instruments to shelter investment gains on college savings.

Managed Accounts

To take full advantage of your 401(k) or similar plan, you must do three things: enroll, save, and invest. As noted above, a growing body of evidence shows that many workers have trouble with each of these steps, and certain provisions of the 2006 pension law are aimed at improving the situation.

As to the first two problems, enrolling and saving, the new law encourages a combination of "opt-out," "step-up," and matching provisions, to boost contributions to 401(k) accounts. A new employee would be automatically enrolled in an account, subject to a 90-day period to opt out. Under the step-up feature, employees would have the share of their salary going into the account raised from a first-year figure of three percent to four in the second year of employment, five percent in the third year, and six percent in the fourth year. Here again the suggested default decision is to automatically raise the share after the first year, subject to an explicit decision by the employee to opt out (by saying no to a higher contribution).

As to matching contributions by employers, the law encourages but, as before, does not require it. The suggested standard is 100 percent matching by the company for the first one percent the employee sets aside, followed by 50 percent matching for the next five percent the employee saves. In all, that's a "recommended" 3.5 percent company match, and a total combined employer-employee contribution of 9.5 percent a year.

What about the third problem, investing? As we noted earlier, participants who do enroll tend to invest in low-risk but low-return assets, to concentrate too much in one or a few types of investment, and to hold too much of their own company's stock. To address these issues, the law encourages business to provide their employees with a choice of either computer-based portfolio management or face-to-face consultations with advisors.

Up until now, many companies offering 401(k) plans have deliberately not given employees advice as to how to diversify or what assets to invest in—for fear of legal liability if the advice is "wrong." Many employees, lacking sufficient guidance or knowledge about investing, tended to leave their funds in secure but low-return assets like money-market funds. Now the 2006 law gives a green light to—and invites—employers to bring in advisors to help employees allocate their savings and diversify their accounts.

In the weeks after the law was passed, this issue of investment advice proved perhaps the most controversial feature. One option recommended in the law is the use of interactive computerized software that employees could use, at least once a year, to compare their asset allocation to some "norm" for an investor in similar circumstances. While inexpensive, this approach might run the risk of leaving out key variables in the employee's larger portfolio of assets, notably holdings outside the 401(k) account.

The second and more controversial (and probably more expensive) path to investment advice involves face-to-face conversations at least annually with financial advisors. Who they would be, and whether they might be accountable to the company, to mutual funds companies, or to anyone else—these are open questions, perhaps to be worked out through further regulations. One early indication is that Fidelity Investments, which manages about one-fourth of the mutual funds in the nation's 401(k) accounts, has come forward with a design to provide free individual consultations with each employee each year for the companies that are its clients. Whether a vested interest on Fidelity's part might skew the kind of advice given is one of the open questions surrounding the issue.

In the meantime, a further feature of the new law tends to bring the story full circle, *i.e.*, it opens the door for 401(k)s to offer, when you retire, the assurance of a guaranteed monthly income—which was, after all, the defining characteristic of traditional defined-benefit pensions. Specifically, the new law gives businesses clarification on something called the "safest available annuity" standard. The hope is that this legal clarification will encourage employers to convert the 401(k) account balances of retiring employees from lump sums to annuities—thereby providing a guaranteed monthly income during their retirement. As with the new rules on account management (which aim to free employees from having to make investment decisions beyond their ken), turning a lump-sum balance into an annuity makes the whole 401(k) approach more like a traditional pension. (Yet another example of such circularities is the cash-balance plan, a hybrid described in Appendix A.)

Tax Treatment of Withdrawals

The tax treatment of 401(k)-type withdrawals can be more complicated than for traditional pension income. As noted in the previous chapter, when traditional pensions are paid out as annuities-for-life, the income usually is taxable under the federal income tax. For defined-contribution or 401(k)-type plans, by contrast, tax treatment of benefits and cash withdrawals depends on the form of income (annuity or lump sum), the amount received, and the beneficiary's age.

Moreover, at the discretion of the employer, traditional pensions can sometimes be taken as a lump-sum payment. Conversely, under the terms of the 2006 Pension Protection Act, 401(k)-type accounts can also be converted from a lump-sum withdrawal into the "safest available annuity." So the lines that used to separate traditional from 401(k)-type payouts and tax treatments are no longer as clear.

Cash Withdrawals — Withdrawals from most qualified company plans usually are not permitted until you reach age 59 ½. Exceptions to this rule vary, so check with your employer. In most cases you can receive payments before 59 ½ if you leave your job, are laid off, are disabled, or can claim "financial hardship" based on the IRS's rather strict definition. You may also be allowed to take an early withdrawal in the form of a loan (see below).

If an early withdrawal is permitted, you will typically (though not always) owe a 10 percent penalty tax on the distribution, in addition to regular income tax. Thus, if you left your job before age 59 ½ and withdrew your entire pension fund in a lump sum of, say, $50,000, you would owe $14,000 in regular Federal income taxes and $5,000 in penalty taxes (assuming you are in the 28 percent tax bracket).

Exceptions to the penalty include withdrawals made on account of your death or disability, for certain medical expenses, if you leave your job or retire at age 55 or over, or as part of an annuity after you leave your job. Early distributions that are rolled over to another pension plan or an IRA within 60 days of your receiving them generally are exempt from both the penalty and regular income tax. Proceed with caution, however, because rollovers must be made carefully to avoid tax complications.

After age 59 ½ there is no legal restriction on making withdrawals from 401(k) and related plans. You will owe income tax on withdrawals that represent either a return of contributions that were not previously taxed or investment earnings. Thus, payouts will be fully taxed. As already noted, however, rollovers are excluded from this tax.

Annuity Benefits — If you convert your 401(k) or other defined-contribution plan into an annuity (as a stream of payments received during your retirement), much and perhaps all of it may be taxable. If the 401(k) was funded entirely with pre-tax dollars (as most are), 100 percent of the annuity income is taxable. Your employer, or the insurance company servicing the annuity, will send you a tax form each year telling you how much of the annuity income is taxable

Lump-Sum Benefits — When you leave your job or retire, your employer may offer you the option of taking your pension in a series of annuity payments or in a single lump sum. A lump-sum payment gives you control over the entire account balance, and you are free to invest it or spend it as you choose. (When it comes to traditional pensions, however, employers are not required to offer you a lump-sum option, and your choice of it may be subject to your employer's approval.)

If you do receive a lump-sum payment, and were born before January 2, 1936, you may be eligible for special income-averaging tax treatment. Whether income averaging will reduce your taxes depends on your regular tax bracket and the special rates applied to averaged income. You should review the tax laws carefully or consult a tax advisor for guidance.

Loans — Some plans allow employees to borrow from their retirement accounts. Such loans are not subject to income tax if they meet certain conditions. The plan must be a qualified pension plan, and the maximum tax-free loan may be limited. In addition, the loan must be repaid within five years, with the important exception of a loan used to buy a principal home, which may be repaid over a much longer period.

Required Distributions — You cannot continue the tax deferral of the funds in your 401(k) account indefinitely. The law requires that you begin taking minimum distributions by a specified date in order to avoid a tax penalty. In most cases, the required date is the later of April 1 of the calendar year following the year in which you turn 70 ½, or April 1 following the year you retire.

The IRS calculates the minimum required distribution according to a pre-determined schedule that treats the account owner's life expectancy as if he or she has a beneficiary who is ten years younger, regardless of whether or not that is actually the case. The rules are different if your spouse is more than ten years your junior and is your sole beneficiary. In that case, the couple can use a joint life expectancy table that captures the younger spouse's age, resulting in a lower required distribution. If you fail to take at least this minimum, you face a tax penalty of 50 percent on the gap between it and what you received.

69

If you are over 59 ½ but under 70 ½, consider the tax and investment consequences of taking withdrawals. The less you withdraw, the longer you avoid paying taxes on the income and the longer you earn tax-free interest. But the larger the account is when you turn 70 ½, the larger will be the required distributions after that. They might be large enough to push you into a higher tax bracket. In that case, you might reduce your total taxes by taking taxable withdrawals earlier, even though you will sacrifice some tax-free investment earnings.

Looking Ahead

Our discussion covers the tax laws most commonly applied to pensions and 401(k)-type accounts. Exemptions and exceptions exist for many laws, especially in the wake of the 2006 Pension Protection Act, as new rules, regulations, and interpretations are crafted before the Act takes full hold in 2008. To understand all your legal options, avoid tax penalties, and minimize your tax bill, you are well-advised to study the laws or consult a competent tax planner. This is especially important if you are faced with financial decisions involving large sums of money (for example, a lump-sum distribution).

It is better to invest in good personalized advice than risk paying higher taxes and possibly tax penalties later on. If you do not plan to retire or change jobs in the near future, the specific tax laws discussed here may change by the time you do retire. Keep abreast of tax and regulatory developments, to help ensure that you use these tax-sheltered investments to your best possible advantage. In the meantime, a good place to keep track of the evolving rules and regulations is the Congressional Budget Office's web site at www.cbo.gov/OnlineTaxGuide. Another official web site on current interpretations and requirements is the U.S. Department of Labor's web site, www.dol.gov/ebsa/faqs.

VII.

"DO-IT-YOURSELF" RETIREMENT ACCOUNTS

MANY people are not covered by a pension plan or will receive benefits too small to meet their financial needs in retirement. Social Security alone provides only a partial and often inadequate replacement of your pre-retirement income. Taking full advantage of 401(k) or other employer-sponsored savings plans can go a long way toward bridging the remaining gap. But for some, especially those who do not have access to employer-sponsored pensions and retirement plans, it may not be enough. If you wish to maintain your pre-retirement standard of living—and beyond that, enjoy the financial independence to pursue lifetime interests after your working years—you should plan to supplement these retirement income sources with additional personal savings.

In recent years Congress has loosened restrictions on Individual Retirement Accounts (IRAs). Eligibility rules have been eased, allowing more Americans to take advantage of these accounts, and contribution limits have been raised. In addition, there are now several types of plans available, including traditional IRAs, Roth IRAs, SIMPLE and SEP plans, Keoghs, and the newest addition, the solo 401(k). Each offers its own distinctive tax benefits. In this chapter, we consider each in turn.

Traditional IRAs

A traditional IRA may be established by anyone under age 70 ½ with earnings. These accounts offer two important tax advantages. The investment income on an IRA contribution accumulates tax-free until the funds are withdrawn. Second, depending on your income and whether you participate in a company pension plan, your IRA contribution may be tax-deductible on Federal and many state income tax returns.

The maximum contribution in 2006 is $4,000 or, if earnings are less than $4,000, 100 percent of income. It increases to $5,000 in 2008. If you file a joint tax return, you and your spouse may each contribute up to the maximum amount as long as your combined earnings cover the contributions. Thus, if one spouse is not working but the other earns at least $8,000 in 2006, each may contribute $4,000 to an IRA. In addition to the maximum contributions, individuals age 50 and older can make an additional annual contribution of up to $1,000 beginning in 2006.

Eligibility for Deductible Contributions

The amount of an IRA contribution that you may deduct from your taxable income depends on (1) your income and (2) whether you are actively participating in an employer's pension plan. If you are not married and are not participating in a retirement plan (or if you are married and neither of you participates in one), you may claim the maximum deduction regardless of your income, assuming your earnings at least equal your contribution.

If you are an employee, the W-2 tax form that your employer gives you every year will indicate in a "Retirement Plan" box whether or not you are an active participant.

Taxpayers covered by a company-sponsored retirement plan cannot deduct their IRA contributions unless their modified adjusted gross income (MAGI) falls below a specific threshold. MAGI can be calculated from your tax return, using the guidelines described in IRS Publication 17. It equals wages, investment earnings, and other income, minus most adjustments to income other than for IRA deductions, plus a few other items, such as deductions for the interest on student loans.

If you are covered by a retirement plan at work, the following rules regarding the effect of modified adjusted gross income on IRA deductibility apply for 2006:

- Single or head of household: Full deduction if MAGI is $50,000 or less, and partial deduction if it is more than $50,000 but less than $60,000. No deduction if MAGI is $60,000 or more.

- Married filing jointly or qualifying widow(er): Full deduction if MAGI is $70,000 or less, and partial deduction if it is more than $75,000 but less than $85,000. No deduction if MAGI is $85,000 or more.

- Married filing separately. Partial deduction if MAGI is less than $10,000 and no deduction if it is $10,000 or more.

If you are *not* covered by a retirement plan at work, a different set of rules apply:

- Single, head of household, or qualifying widow(er): Full deduction, regardless of income.

- Married filing jointly or separately with a spouse who is not covered by a plan at work: Full deduction, regardless of income.

- Married filing jointly with a spouse who is covered by a plan at work: Full deduction if MAGI is $150,000 or less, and partial deduction if it is more than $150,000 and less than $160,000. No deduction if MAGI is $160,000 or more.

- Married filing separately with a spouse who is covered by a plan at work. Partial deduction if MAGI is less than $10,000 and no deduc-

72

tion if it is $10,000 or more.

Finally, if you did not live with your spouse at any time during the year, your filing status is considered single and your IRA deduction is determined accordingly.

The MAGI limits on deductibility and phase-out ranges are scheduled to increase over the next several years. In 2007, for example, married taxpayers who file jointly and are covered by a retirement plan at work will be able to receive the full deduction if their income is $80,000 or less.

Deductible and nondeductible contributions for any given tax year may be made up until income-tax day (usually April 15) of the following year. Of course, you will benefit most from the tax-free buildup of investment earnings if you invest early rather than waiting until the last minute.

Should You Contribute to a Non-Deductible IRA?

If you are not eligible to deduct your contribution, you can still make a nondeductible contribution. If a deduction of less than the maximum amount is allowed, you may make a nondeductible contribution, provided that your total IRA contributions do not exceed the allowable maximum.

However, if your income level makes you eligible to contribute to a Roth IRA (discussed below), you are almost certainly better off doing that. Investment earnings in both types of accounts accumulate free of tax. The earnings in a traditional IRA are taxed upon withdrawal, however, while withdrawals from a Roth IRA, if certain conditions are met, are completely tax-free. In addition, you are not required to take minimum distributions from a Roth IRA after you reach age 70 ½, as you are with traditional IRAs. In short, greater tax benefits and more lenient withdrawal rules make Roth IRAs a better alternative to traditional but nondeductible IRAs.

However, until 2010, Roth IRAs are subject to income limits. If your income level is high enough to bar you from contributing to a Roth IRA, a traditional but nondeductible IRA still offers the tax-free buildup of investment earnings.

For most investors age 59 ½ or older, there is little downside to making nondeductible contributions, since there is no penalty for withdrawals. You can make contributions through age 70 ½, after which you must begin drawing down your account.

For investors who expect to be in relatively high tax brackets when they withdraw funds from a nondeductible IRA account, the tax treatment of investment earnings is another consideration. The investment buildup in an IRA is taxed, upon withdrawal, as ordinary income at rates as high as 35 percent. In contrast, long-term capital gains on non-IRA investments are subject to a maximum tax of 15 percent.

By investing inside an IRA, you also miss out on the benefit of the new, lower tax on "qualified" dividends. Since 2003, qualified dividends are subject to the same 5 percent or 15 percent maximum tax rate that applies to net capital gains. If your regular tax rate is 25 percent or higher, the tax rate on qualified dividends is 15 percent. If your regular tax rate is lower than 25 percent, the 5 percent rate applies.

To qualify for this tax treatment, the dividends must have been paid by a U.S. corporation or a qualified foreign corporation. You (or the mutual fund you invest in) must meet a holding-period requirement.

By contrast, mutual fund dividends attributable to income from real estate investment trusts (REITS), money market securities, taxable or tax-exempt bonds, and some preferred and foreign stocks are taxed at higher, ordinary income rates.

Any investment buildup you withdraw is taxable income. So investing inside an IRA means that you convert favorably-taxed capital gains and qualified dividends into ordinary income, which receives less favorable tax treatment. If you expect the buildup of your investment to come primarily from unrealized long-term capital gains and qualified dividends, you may be better off placing your funds in a conventional account rather than a nondeductible IRA. The gains will not be taxed until they are realized. At that point they will be subject to the lower tax on capital gains and qualified dividends rather than the higher tax on ordinary income. In addition, you will be able to deduct capital losses, which you cannot do within a nondeductible IRA.

A conventional account is also likely to be more advantageous than a nondeductible IRA if you (or your mutual fund manager) follow a "buy and hold" strategy. If, in contrast, your account will have a high rate of portfolio turnover, a nondeductible IRA may be a better choice, because it allows capital gains to compound tax deferred.

If you do make nondeductible contributions, it is up to you to keep a record of them. Most banks, brokers, and other IRA trustees report withdrawals as if they are fully taxable. It is your responsibility to show otherwise and thus avoid paying a double tax when nondeductible contributions (which you've already paid taxes on) are withdrawn. For some people, the more complicated bookkeeping involved when one has nondeductible IRAs may outweigh the benefits.

Restrictions and Penalties

Deferred taxes on contributions and investment earnings make traditional, deductible IRAs a very attractive investment. To encourage their use *specifically for retirement planning* rather than short-term investing, and to insure that IRA funds actually are drawn upon for retirement income and not simply used to build up tax-sheltered legacies, certain restrictions apply to the use of IRA funds.

Before you reach age 59 ½ there are no legal restrictions on withdrawals from IRAs. This is in contrast to 401(k)s and other company pension plans, where early withdrawals are generally prohibited. However, early IRA withdrawals almost always are subject to a 10 percent *penalty* tax, plus regular income tax on the portion that reflects the return of tax-deductible contributions and investment earnings.

The only exception to both the income tax and the penalty is for a payment that is repaid or rolled over into another tax-sheltered account within 60 days. This includes loans that are repaid within 60 days. (Longer "loans" are treated as taxable distributions.)

There are several other exceptions to the penalty for early IRA withdrawals. The penalty is waived if you are totally disabled; if you pay deductible medical expenses that exceed 7.5 percent of your adjusted gross income (in which case the IRA penalty does not apply to distributions that exceed the 7.5 percent threshold); or if you received unemployment benefits for at least 12 consecutive weeks and you paid medical insurance premiums for yourself or your family (withdrawals up to the amount paid for insurance are not penalized).

If you are a first-time home buyer, up to $10,000 may be withdrawn without penalty to cover qualifying home-buyer expenses. Distributions are also free of penalty if they are used to pay for the expenses of a higher education, including tuition, room, and board for yourself or your family. If you die before reaching age 59 ½, the assets in your traditional IRA can be distributed to your beneficiary or to your estate without either having to pay the 10 percent additional tax.

Finally, the IRA penalty is waived for an early distribution that is part of a series of roughly equal payments received yearly over your life expectancy (or the joint life expectancy of you and a beneficiary). In other words, it is waived for payments received as an annuity.

As with many "targeted tax breaks," there are many rules and regulations governing these exemptions. If you think you may be eligible for one, check the tax laws first to make sure you cover all the bases.

The expanding list of penalty exemptions makes IRAs a more liquid investment than they used to be for people under age 59 ½. However, just because you qualify to make a penalty-free withdrawal does not mean you should do so. Every withdrawal reduces your potential to build wealth using these tax-favored accounts. In general, early withdrawals should be avoided.

Between ages 59 ½ and 70 ½ there is no tax penalty for withdrawals, but they are taxed as ordinary income. If you made both deductible and nondeductible IRA contributions, part of any distribution will be tax-free (see "Record Keeping," below). Until you reach age 70 ½ you are not required to withdraw funds, and the longer you leave your investments intact the longer you will enjoy the tax-free buildup of investment earnings. However, if the distributions you will eventually be required to take will be so large as to push you into a higher tax bracket, consider withdrawing some funds before age 70 ½ even if you do not "need" the money; in this way, you may smooth your tax bill.

After age 70 ½ you must begin drawing down your IRA account. After April 1 following the end of the year in which you turn 70 ½, no further contributions may be made (except for lump-sum distributions from company pension plans) and you must begin receiving minimum annual distributions, based on IRS guidelines. Failure to take the minimum distribution may result in a 50 percent penalty tax on the required amount not actually distributed.

Under the old method of calculating required minimum distributions, you had to choose one of the methods recognized by the IRS for calculating the required minimum withdrawal. Once the choice was made it was difficult to revoke, and each method carried important implications for your taxes, your beneficiaries, and your estate. Under rules that became effective in 2001, the account owner's beneficiary selection made at the required beginning date is no longer irrevocable, so you can change beneficiaries as the need arises. And the IRS now bases required minimum distribution calculations on the account owner's age, less ten years (unless a spousal beneficiary is more than ten years younger).

In most cases, the new rules result in smaller required distributions, and longer deferral periods. They also make estate planning more predictable.

Roth IRAs

Roth IRAs became available in 1998. Unlike traditional IRAs, contributions to Roth IRAs are not deductible. But the investment earnings grow tax-free and, subject to certain conditions, withdrawals may be completely tax-free. Thus, an owner of a Roth IRA will never have to pay tax on the IRA's earnings (unless he or she takes early withdrawals, as discussed below).

76

As a matter of estate-planning, Roth IRAs do *not* require minimum distributions at age 70 ½. Investors thus have the option of continuing to let the full balance of the IRA compound tax-free. Moreover, Roth IRAs may still be funded after the taxpayer reaches age 70 ½, unlike traditional IRAs. The income caps that govern contribution limits are also higher than for a regular IRA.

An individual may make nondeductible contributions to a Roth IRA of up to $4,000 per year ($5,000 for those age 50 and older) in 2006, or, if earnings are less than that, 100 percent of earned income. Couples filing a joint return may contribute up to $4,000 each providing their combined income is at least $8,000. The $4,000 limit is reduced by any deductible or nondeductible contributions made to a traditional IRA.

In other words, combined contributions to traditional and Roth IRAs may not exceed $4,000 per year. Roth IRAs may still be funded after you reach age 70 ½, so long as you have the required compensation.

Under current law, the maximum contribution amount increases to $5,000 in 2008 for those under age 50. For those 50 and older, it increases to $6,000.

Depending on your income, your maximum contribution may be less than $4,000 or even zero. "Income" here refers to "modified adjusted gross income" (MAGI) as defined by the IRS specifically for figuring Roth eligibility. For single and head of household filers or married couples filing separately who lived apart the entire year, permissible contributions are phased out for MAGIs between $95,000 and $110,000. For married couples filing jointly, contributions are phased out for MAGIs between $150,000 and $160,000. For a married couple filing separately who lived with each other for any part of the year, the phaseout range is $0 to $10,000.

No Roth contributions are permitted for income above the maximum thresholds. Unlike traditional IRAs, these income phase-outs are the same, regardless of whether you (or your spouse) are covered by an employer's pension plan.

Contributions for a given tax year may be made up until income-tax day (usually April 15) of the following year. There is a 6 percent penalty tax each year for contributions that exceed the limit, unless the excess plus any related investment earnings are withdrawn by the time you file your tax return.

Converting a Traditional IRA to a Roth IRA

Converting a traditional IRA to a Roth IRA, in order to take advantage of the tax-free withdrawal provision, is also possible. You may do this if your modified adjusted gross income is $100,000 or less and you are not in the category of married-filing-separately. (For this purpose, MAGI does not include the amount of the conversion.) However, you must pay income taxes on the amount converted.

Converting could appeal to taxpayers *who plan to leave their IRAs to their heirs*, since distributions to beneficiaries often will be tax-free. However, the conversion tax should be carefully considered. The additional income from the conversion can boost taxpayers into a higher tax bracket, or make Social Security benefits taxable as a result of the increase in income. If you do make a conversion, you should try to pay the tax from sources outside the IRA.

To make a conversion, the accountholder can direct the trustee of the traditional IRA to transfer the funds to a new Roth IRA trustee, or simply register the new account with the same trustee. Funds can also be transferred by taking a distribution from the IRA and rolling it over to the Roth IRA.

SEP (Simplified Employee Pensions) accounts are also eligible for conversion to Roth IRAs, as are SIMPLE IRAs (discussed below), provided you have held the SIMPLE IRA account for at least 2 years.

If you are under age 59 ½, a conversion from a traditional IRA to a Roth IRA is not subject to the 10 percent tax penalty for early distributions.

Recharacterizations

If you convert a traditional IRA to a Roth IRA and decide you want to "undo" it (perhaps because you discover that your income is more than the $100,000 ceiling), you can transfer the funds back into a regular IRA by doing a "recharacterization." You can also do this if, for example, you contributed to a Roth and later decide you would like to switch your contribution to a regular IRA in order to claim a deduction. Recharacterizations may be done until the due date for your taxes (usually April 15, plus any extensions).

A traditional IRA that is converted to a Roth IRA then recharacterized back to a traditional IRA may be "reconverted" back into a Roth. The main reason to do this is to save on taxes in the event the value of the converted funds declines. Instead of paying taxes on the higher value of the funds as of the first conversion to a Roth, you can pay the tax based on their lower value when you reconvert. However, the IRS has placed limits on the number and timing of reconversions.

Improper switches between IRA funds can trigger taxes and penalties for early withdrawals and excess contributions. To avoid unpleasant surprises, consult IRS Publications 17 and 590 or your tax advisor.

Withdrawals

The investment earnings on your Roth contributions accumulate free of tax. Withdrawals are completely tax-free *if* they are "qualified." To be considered qualified, they must be made after the account has been held for at least 5 years and the taxpayer is older than 59 ½, disabled, a beneficiary receiving distributions following the death of the account owner, or using the distribution to pay up to $10,000 for the expenses of buying a first home.

The 5-year holding period begins with January 1 of the first tax-year you contribute to a Roth IRA. If you subsequently open other Roth accounts, you do not have to meet separate 5-year tests for them. For example, if you opened your first Roth IRA by making a $500 contribution in March 2000 for the 1999 tax year, and in 2001 you converted a traditional IRA into another Roth IRA, the 5-year holding period for both accounts began January 1, 1999 and ended December 31, 2003.

Even if a distribution is not qualified, the first withdrawals from the account are treated as a return of the investor's contribution and are tax-free. After amounts equal to the entire contribution have been withdrawn, additional withdrawals are taxable. All of your Roth accounts are treated as one account for purposes of figuring whether any withdrawal is a tax-free return of your contributions.

If a withdrawal is taxable *and* you are under age 59 ½, it is also subject to a 10 percent penalty. The exceptions to this early-withdrawal penalty are the same as for traditional IRAs. Namely, it is waived if you are disabled, have medical expenses exceeding 7.5 percent of adjusted gross income, received unemployment benefits for at least 12 weeks and paid medical insurance premiums, or you paid first-time home expenses up to $10,000.

If you have a Roth IRA that was created by converting a traditional IRA, the rules on the taxation of withdrawals are somewhat different. For example, a distribution taken before age 59 ½ may qualify as a tax-free return of your contribution but still be subject to the 10 percent penalty. See IRS Publication 590 for further details.

Distributions to Beneficiaries

If you *inherit* a Roth IRA, you must begin taking minimum distributions each year, unless you are a surviving spouse. They may or may not be taxable, as discussed below.

You must take distributions according to your life expectancy or else withdraw the entire account by the end of the fifth year following the owner's death. However, if you are a surviving spouse and you are the account's sole beneficiary, you may avoid this requirement by electing to treat the account as your own, in which case you are not required to take any distributions during your lifetime.

Surviving spouses who choose to take distributions over their life expectancy can delay the first withdrawal until the date the original account owner would have turned 70 ½. The choice of distribution method may not be up to the beneficiary, as the original owner of the account or the terms of the plan may specify which method is to be used (so you should check this before opening a Roth IRA).

Distributions to surviving beneficiaries are tax-free if they are received five years or more after the original account owner opened his first Roth account. Before that 5-year period, distributions are tax-free to the extent they represent a return of contributions. After amounts equal to the entire contribution have been withdrawn, additional withdrawals are taxable.

There is no 10 percent penalty for early withdrawals from a Roth IRA if you receive them as a beneficiary, even if you are under age 59 ½.

Keep in mind that while Roth IRAs may be subject to more favorable tax treatment at death than traditional IRAs, they must also be included as an asset in your estate for tax purposes. In 2006, the federal estate tax applies to taxable estates of more than $2 million.

Roth IRAs vs. Traditional IRAs

The confusing rules for IRAs and Roth IRAs can be overwhelming when you are trying to decide which is the best way to save for retirement. *Before putting funds in either, consider putting money into a 401(k) or other employer-sponsored plan.* If your employer makes matching contribution these plans are an all but unbeatable investment, and you should fund them at least up to the amount the employer matches.

Next, determine your eligibility for IRA contributions. Factors to consider are your income, marital status, and whether you or your spouse is active in a pension plan. High earners who are barred from making deductible contributions to a traditional IRA may still be eligible to open a Roth account, because the income caps are higher. On the other hand, a nonworking spouse of a high earner may be barred from contributing to a Roth IRA but be eligible to deduct a contribution to a standard IRA. In short, the eligibility rules may make your choice clearer.

If you are eligible to contribute to both a deductible traditional IRA and a Roth IRA, your decision is more difficult. Is it better to pay taxes now (on a Roth contribution) or later (on withdrawals from a traditional IRA)?

As a rule of thumb, if you expect your marginal tax rate to be higher when you withdraw the money, a Roth IRA is generally a better bet. If you expect your rate to be lower, a traditional IRA will provide a higher return.

The problem, of course, is that nobody knows what tax rates will be in the future. In light of large and growing federal budget deficits, however, it would seem prudent to expect eventual income-tax rate increases down the road. To that extent, Roth IRAs become more attractive. The reasoning is that you pay a historically low rate now when putting after-tax money into the Roth. Then when you withdraw money later (when tax rates may well be higher), the withdrawals will be tax-free.

Nevertheless, investors reportedly have shied away from Roth IRAs in favor of the up-front deductibility of traditional IRAs because they are afraid Congress will someday change the rules and make future withdrawals taxable. This is always a risk with any tax-sheltered account. Tax laws change often. However, the recent trend has been toward creating more tax breaks, not eliminating them. Congress also may create more retirement tax breaks in hopes of reducing the looming fiscal burden of aging baby boomers on Social Security, Medicare, and other age-based government programs.

If so, one might expect the future to hold an even more complicated federal tax code, plus higher tax rates.

In any case, and as already noted, you are not required to take distributions from your Roth IRA at any age. This makes them more flexible than standard IRAs and also makes them an attractive tool for estate planning.

Setting Up an IRA

Many financial institutions offer IRA investments. These are technically "trust" or "custodial" accounts with the institution serving as the trustee or custodian. In addition, insurance companies offer deferred annuities that qualify as IRAs. You often have the option of investing your contributions among a number of separate funds (say, a selection of mutual funds). Before establishing any account, carefully review the terms of the agreement, including any management fees and restrictions on investments or transfers of the funds. Try to arrange to pay annual management fees separately so that they will not be deducted from the IRA account itself.

IRA funds may be invested by their trustee or custodian, per your instructions, in a wide range of vehicles, from a bank CD to a diverse selection of mutual funds. Your investment options may depend on the terms of the account. For example, if your IRA is invested in a CD at your local bank, you cannot readily switch to a mutual stock fund unless you change custodians. On the other hand, if your IRA is with an investment company such as

Vanguard or Fidelity, you will have a huge array of investment choices.

Tax laws do not restrict the direct transfer of funds from one IRA acccount to another, and thus they allow you considerable flexibility in changing custodians (*e.g.*, switching from a bank to Fidelity, or from Fidelity to Vanguard). If done properly (competent advice should be obtained beforehand), such a transfer is not considered a "rollover," and the usual limit of one rollover per year (see below) does not apply. However, transfers may be limited by a trustee, depending on the term of the agreement, so it is important to review these terms beforehand.

If you prefer to take a more active hand in managing your investments, you can bypass the traditional IRA and set up a "self-directed" IRA through a broker or bank. This type of account retains the bank as trustee or custodian, but allows the investor to select the investments. The U.S. Treasury provides model trust and custodial account forms that satisfy all IRS requirements for such accounts. It is up to you to find an institution that will agree to serve as trustee. IRA accounts currently held in other forms can be converted to self-directed accounts with no tax penalty. Such conversions must meet certain requirements to escape taxation and should be done with care. In any event, the range of investment options available through traditional IRAs is more than adequate for most investors.

Rollovers

You can make a tax-free rollover of funds from another IRA or from a qualified retirement plan (such as a 401(k) into an IRA, in which case there is no limit on the amount transferred. To avoid income taxes or penalties, you should get competent advice before doing this. If the funds are paid to you before being re-deposited, there is a limit of one tax-free rollover per year and, to qualify, the rollover must be made within 60 days. If the funds are directly transferred from one account to another, there is no restriction on the number of times you can make tax-free switches.

In the case of lump-sum distributions from a 401(k) account, for example, funds that you plan to roll into an IRA should be transferred directly to the new account rather than paid out to you, to avoid tax complications.

Record Keeping

Because IRAs receive special tax treatment, and because this treatment is subject to change over the years, it is important to keep a record of all contributions and withdrawals. To minimize tax complications, IRAs based on your own contributions should be kept separate from an IRA based on a lump-sum distribution from a 401(k) or other employer-sponsored plan. Accounts based on deductible contributions should be kept separate from accounts based on nondeductible contributions.

In the eyes of the IRS, all IRAs are treated as a single account, and withdrawals in a given year from any and all IRAs are treated as a single withdrawal. Therefore, if you have IRAs based on both deductible and nondeductible contributions, a portion of any withdrawal will be taxable and another portion will be tax free. This "ratio tax" applies even to a withdrawal from a separate IRA based wholly on nondeductible contributions. IRA trustees (such as banks) will report all withdrawals to the IRS *as if they are taxable*. The burden of proving that they are not is upon you. According to the IRS, you should keep extensive tax records from the time you make contributions until all IRA savings are withdrawn.

SIMPLE, SEP, and Keogh Plans

Small businesses and the self-employed often cannot afford the expense of setting up and maintaining a traditional retirement plan. Two alternatives are the SIMPLE (Saving Incentive Match Plan for Employees) and the SEP (Simplified Employee Pension). These are hybrids of a company retirement plan and an IRA. Before 1997, businesses with fewer than 25 employees could set up 401(k)-type SEPs for them—and some of these plans are still in effect. Beginning in 1997, however, salary-reduction SEPs for employees have been replaced by SIMPLEs.

The maximum amount that can be contributed by employees each year to a SIMPLE IRA is $10,000 in 2006. Employers are obligated to match the contribution up to a limit of three percent of the employee's wages or to make a fixed contribution of two percent for every employee. A SIMPLE plan can permit participants age 50 and older to make catch-up contributions. The catch-up contribution limit is $2,500 in 2006.

The tax laws regarding withdrawals are generally the same as those that apply to IRAs, with one notable exception. For the first two years of an employee's participation, any withdrawal before age 59 ½ that is subject to an early withdrawal penalty is penalized at a rate of 25 percent (in addition to regular income taxes) rather than 10 percent. After this two-year period the penalty is 10 percent.

The maximum amount of salary that may be contributed by an employee to a salary-reduction SEP is $15,000 in 2006. The $15,000 figure is subject to cost-of-living increases after 2006. A plan can permit participants age 50 and older to make additional catch-up contributions of up to $5,000 in 2006. Cost-of-living adjustments begin after that. The tax laws regarding withdrawals are generally the same as those that apply to standard IRAs.

Another type of simplified employee pension called a SEP-IRA is used mainly by the self-employed. If you operate a small business, you can make contributions to a traditional individual retirement arrangement for yourself (and, technically, for each eligible employee). A SEP-IRA is controlled by the owner of the account. Contributions must be based on a written allocation formula and may not discriminate in favor of highly-compensated employees. The maximum contribution for 2006 cannot exceed the lesser of 25 percent of compensation (20 percent for the self-employed) or $44,000. Special rules apply for maximum contributions made by the employer.

Keogh retirement accounts may be set up by a sole proprietor or a partnership. These plans allow the self-employed, and in some cases those working for them, to make tax-deductible contributions, up to maximum limits that vary depending on the plan but generally may not exceed the lesser of 100 percent of compensation or $44,000 in 2006. As with SEPs and other qualified plans, investment earnings on all contributions accrue tax-free until withdrawals are made.

Keoghs can be created as defined-benefit plans, but most are defined-contribution plans. The funds may be invested however the self-employed individual (or the employer, in the case of a small business) chooses, much like an IRA. If a Keogh is designed as a defined-benefit plan, the targeted annual retirement benefit can be as high as $170,000. Each year's contribution must be calculated by an actuary.

Withdrawals from Keogh accounts are subject to restrictions, taxes, and early withdrawal penalties similar to those that apply to other qualified company retirement plans; for specific guidelines, consult a tax advisor.

Solo 401(k)s

The solo 401(k) is a new variation of the corporate 401(k) plans that have been around for more than 20 years. It was introduced in the Economic Growth and Tax Relief Reconciliation Act of 2001, which took effect in January 2002.

Using a solo 401(k), a business consisting of only an owner (or an owner and his or her spouse) can make greater tax-deductible contributions than under a SEP IRA or SIMPLE IRA, and at lower income levels. Contributions are discretionary, so owners can vary them from year to year or skip them altogether.

In 2006, total contributions to a solo 401(k) cannot exceed 100 percent of pay, up to a maximum of $44,000 for those under age 50 and $49,000 for those age 50 and older. This amount includes salary deferrals of up to $14,000 ($18,000 if age 50 or older), *plus* an employer contribution of up to 25 percent of pay (or 20 percent of self-employment income).

While SEP-IRA contributions also max out at $44,000, they are limited to 25 percent of pay (more to the point, 20 percent for the self-employed). And, SEP IRAs do not provide for additional catch-up contributions. With a SIMPLE IRA, the amount that can be deferred is $10,000 this year, or up to $12,500 for those age 50 or older, plus three percent of income (measured as total business income minus half the self-employment tax).

In practice, these rules mean that a self-employed person with an income of $100,000 could defer over $33,000 this year using a solo 401(k). By contrast, the limit for a SEP IRA at the same income would be under $19,000, and for a SIMPLE IRA, under $13,000.

In short, the ability to make generous contributions at lower income levels with a solo 401(k) means that business owners who want to catch-up on retirement contributions can do so more quickly than they could with a SEP IRA or a SIMPLE IRA.

One group that will not find these plans appealing is businesses that have employees, or those that anticipate adding them. Contributions are 100 percent vested immediately, and an owner who gives himself the maximum employer contribution is required to contribute the maximum for employees.

Making the Choice

If you are self-employed in a small business, your choices for tax-favored retirement planning using tax-free contributions come down to IRAs (both traditional and Roth), SIMPLE IRAs, SEPs, Keoghs, and the solo 401(k). IRAs generally are least advantageous since the contribution limits are small. A competent advisor can help you decide among a SIMPLE IRA, a SEP (other than salary-reduction types, which have been replaced by SIMPLE IRAs), or a more complicated Keogh or solo 401(k).

SEP accounts may be opened and funded as late as the due date of your return (usually April 15th) following the end of the tax year, whereas Keoghs and solo 401(k)s must be opened by December 31st, although funding can be postponed until April. For more information see IRS Publication 560 *Retirement Plans for Small Business*.

Caution

As with pension plans, the tax laws pertaining to IRAs, SEPs, and Keoghs are complex. *Many employer-sponsored retirement accounts eventually end up in IRAs*, and these accounts will be the largest financial asset that many individuals own. Thus, it is especially important to obtain competent advice regarding such things as the naming of beneficiaries and the calculation of required minimum distributions. It also is important to seek advice on estate planning, since IRAs (and other retirement accounts) can add substantially to the value of an estate.

VIII.
GUIDELINES FOR RETIREMENT INVESTING

ONCE you have an idea of how much you will need to save for retirement and the available retirement saving options, the next step is to devise an asset allocation and investment strategy. It is beyond the scope of this discussion to describe the panorama of investment philosophies, as well as the fast-growing roster of securities and products available to investors. But a few key principles of investing provide a starting point for building a sound, sensible portfolio.

In this chapter, the principles to be explored are the balancing of risk and return, diversification of assets, the use of tax-efficient strategies, and dollar cost averaging.[1]

Asset Allocation

Studies have shown that the way investors allocate their assets, rather than individual security selection, has the greatest influence on overall returns. Deciding how to allocate and invest your assets will depend largely on the level of risk you need to take to reach your savings goal, and, just as important, how much risk you feel comfortable taking.

"Safe" investments, such as short-term certificates of deposit, typically provide lower yields over the long run than a diversified portfolio that includes stocks, even though the latter may be subject to more short-term volatility. Stocks and stock funds, while volatile in the short-term, have historically provided the best opportunity for long-term growth over most time periods. Retirees and those saving for retirement should have some money in them to help prevent price inflation from eroding the value of their savings.

However, not everyone feels comfortable about investing heavily in the stock market. One widely used rule of thumb to determine how much to invest in stocks is to subtract your age from 100. So, for example, if you are 30 years old, this guideline suggests you should have about 70 percent of your money in the stock market. But that is just a starting point, not the last word. If you are a 30-year old whose stomach turns at the thought of losing money, forget traditional wisdom. The same holds true for a 60-year old with a generous pension and other assets who may feel restricted by having 40 percent of his money in stocks, since he can afford to take more risk.

While there are no hard-and-fast rules about how to allocate your assets,

---

[1] For a more thorough discussion of investment issues, see the AIER book *How to Invest Wisely*.

several considerations go into making that determination. The longer you have until retirement, the more risk you can afford to take because you presumably have the ability to wait out short-term market fluctuations. Also, consider your financial picture as a whole, rather than seeing each account as a separate entity. If you have a lot of employer stock in a 401(k) plan, for example, it probably is not a good idea to invest in that stock, or stocks in the same industry sector, for your IRA. If you tend to invest conservatively in a tax-deferred retirement account, you might wish to invest more aggressively in accounts outside the plan.

Perhaps most importantly, consider your tolerance for risk. When it comes to investing, risk and reward are always a tradeoff. The more risk you take, the more reward you stand to reap over the long term. The key to successful investing is balancing the level of risk you can prudently take to reach your goals with the emotional tug of losing money from time to time.

One way to control risk is to diversify your holdings. Most investors would do better, for example, by holding a mutual fund that tracks the S&P 500 index than trying to pick stocks or actively managed mutual funds. The reason is that such funds have very low expenses and they hold many more issues (500) than an actively managed portfolio.

For further diversification, many individuals may wish to follow what has been called "asset class investing." This approach takes advantage of the fact that various segments of the market have dissimilar price movements. Stocks and bonds are the two broadest segments, but much research has shown that the stock segment can be sliced into additional segments, some of which have had higher returns than the S&P 500. The short-term volatility of these segments is larger than it is for the S&P 500; but, when they are included in an investment portfolio, the volatility of that portfolio's return will usually be less than the average of its components.

What kind of asset classes should an investor in stocks choose? Brokerage firms and mutual fund management companies often create funds simply to have "new products." But many of these (such as industry-specific funds) are not suitable for an asset class investor. In general, the *size* (large cap or small cap) and the *valuation* (growth or value) of the stocks within various funds account for most of the variation in their returns.

In sum, investors who wish to diversify their stock holdings beyond the S&P 500 might consider a mix that includes, say, a large cap growth fund, a large cap value fund, and a small cap value fund. Some investors may also wish to hold a small part of their portfolios—perhaps 5 to 10 percent—in assets that have low or no correlation to the stock or bond markets, such as real estate investment trusts (REITs) or precious metals.

An increasingly popular retirement investment option, called life-cycle funds, claims broad appeal as an easy, one-stop solution to retirement planning. Also called target-date funds, they allocate assets into different fund baskets based on specific retirement years, such as 2010, 2015, or 2030. The initial mix, which may include stock funds, bond funds, and perhaps real estate or international funds, shifts to more conservative allocations as retirement approaches and usually becomes even more conservative after the target date passes.

But these funds also have some obvious drawbacks. They do not take into account individual circumstances, such as whether someone plans to retire early, wants to leave an inheritance, or has other sources of retirement income. They may not include asset classes with a strong negative correlation to the stock market, such as commodity or real estate funds. And they usually tie investors down to using just one fund family across all asset classes. Still, those who do not have the time or inclination to manage and monitor their own investments may find them preferable to assembling a diversified portfolio themselves.

Remember that asset allocation is a continual process. As markets fluctuate, you will need to *rebalance your account* at least once a year to bring it into line with your asset allocation strategy. While it may be tempting to leave stock market gains on the table rather than transfer them to the more conservative side your investment balance sheet, spreading your bets by rebalancing will help cushion the impact of a market downturn.

As noted, index funds have minimal costs and expenses. Ample research has shown that most actively-managed mutual funds fail to consistently "beat the indexes." If you are going to invest in stocks and bond funds, *low-cost index funds* are an excellent way to limit your expenses.

Saving in a Taxable versus Tax-Exempt Account

Not everyone saves for retirement exclusively in a tax-deferred qualified retirement plan. Because contributions to such plans are usually derived from earnings, money you receive from another source, such as an inheritance or substantial monetary gifts, may need to be placed into a taxable account. Or you might invest through taxable accounts because you want to contribute more than your retirement plans permit.

Some investors prefer to use taxable accounts for at least part of their retirement savings because capital gains and dividends earned on stocks are now taxed at a maximum rate of 15 percent. As the previous chapter mentioned, if you hold the stocks in a traditional IRA, 401(k) or other qualified retirement plan, you pay ordinary income tax rates of as much as 35 percent when you withdraw the money. (This doesn't apply to Roth IRAs, which permit tax-free withdrawals.) Also, withdrawals from 401(k) plans count toward taxable income when the government calculates the extent to which Social Security benefits will be taxed. By contrast, the sale of stocks or other assets does not affect the taxation of Social Security benefits.

Another advantage to saving in a taxable account is the ability to deduct capital losses. Investors can offset capital gains and losses evenly with no limit. Thus, if you sold a stock this year for a gain of $20,000, you could use a loss of $20,000 from the sale of other securities to absorb the entire gain, resulting in no tax. If your capital losses for one year exceed your gains, leaving you with a net capital loss, you can typically subtract as much as $3,000 of that loss ($1,500 if married and filing separately from your spouse) from wages and other ordinary income. You can carry losses greater than the limit into future years.

At the same time, the fact that capital gains are not taxed in tax-deferred retirement accounts can create the temptation to "take a flier" with such funds, say, by investing in high-risk "growth stocks" paying little or no dividends. While the prospect of not paying gains taxes on a stock that increases markedly in price might seem to appear sound, all too often such stocks decline toward worthlessness. In that event, the investor is often chagrined to find he cannot deduct the loss (conveniently forgetting that he received a deduction when funds were paid into the account) and holds on to "losers" in the account in hopes of recovery. The problem is that even the "miracle" of compound interest cannot make zero increase to more than zero.

As a solution, some investors reserve the majority of tax-deferred retirement plans for conservative holdings that offer generous current yields, which can compound and accumulate free of tax. They use their taxable accounts for more aggressive investments to retain the ability to deduct losses and to avoid turning capital gains into income.

The treatment of capital gains and losses should be only one factor in considering whether to consider using more aggressive investments in a taxable account, however. Regardless of tax benefits, a bad investment is a bad investment.

Using Tax-Efficient Investments

If you use taxable accounts, be aware of the tax ramifications of various types of investments. Interest income from securities such as certificates of deposit or taxable bonds is taxed at high ordinary income rates. The increase in the face value of Treasury Inflation-Protected Securities (TIPs) is federally taxable as income in the year it accrues, even though you do not actually receive it until the bond matures. This feature makes them more suitable for tax-deferred retirement accounts as well. On the other hand, income from Series EE and Series I savings bonds is not taxed until the bonds are cashed, making them ideal for those who wish to defer paying taxes on the accumulated interest until after they retire.

As a general rule, *you do not want to put a tax-sheltered investment into a tax-sheltered account*. For example, municipal bonds issued by state and local government agencies are generally better for taxable accounts because the interest on them is exempt from federal (and sometimes state) income taxes. Although the rate of return on munis is lower than the return on comparable taxable bonds, their after-tax yields are often higher, particularly if you are in a high tax bracket. Similarly, the tax-free compounding of earnings in deferred annuities becomes redundant if placed in a qualified retirement plan, making these more suitable for taxable accounts as well.

People investing in mutual funds in a taxable account should consider the tax efficiency of their investments. If possible, you should minimize or avoid the use of investments that generate taxable income or short-term capital gains, which are taxed at high ordinary income rates. This may not be as easy as it sounds because of the quirky nature of mutual fund taxes.

When you buy a stock, you do not incur a short- or long-term capital gains tax until you sell it (although you may incur taxes on any dividends the shares produce). Not so with mutual funds, which have what are called "capital-gains distributions." If you have money outside a tax-deferred retirement plan, you can be hit with a capital gains distribution even if you don't sell your mutual fund shares.

That's because the fund manager is busily buying and selling securities in the portfolio. If stocks have appreciated since their purchase and were held for one year or less the profit could be taxed as a short-term capital gain and distributed to current shareholders. This could occur even in a year when the fund has lost money.

Certain types of stock funds, such as index funds or those with the words "tax managed" in their names, try to minimize or avoid the generation of taxable income and short-term capital gains. Exchange-traded funds (ETFs), which have investment characteristics similar to a mutual fund but trade like a stock, can also offer the potential for greater tax efficiency than most mutual funds.

Dollar-Cost Averaging

People who are saving for retirement through a 401(k), IRA, or other tax-deferred plan usually do so gradually, either through periodic payroll deductions or their own contributions. Those who invest on their own in a taxable account often do so through regular, automatic transfers from their bank accounts into mutual funds. In either case, they are, in effect, using a strategy called dollar-cost averaging.

Dollar-cost averaging is simply putting the same amount of money into an investment on a regular schedule regardless of what is happening to the price. The idea is to take advantage of price volatility; fewer shares will be purchased when prices are high, and more will be purchased when prices are low. Depending on market trends, it can lower your average cost per share. The discipline of automatic investing every month is also, in and of itself, helpful to many investors.

Consistency is the key word here. You cannot decide to bail out when the market turns down and start over again when it gets better. That would be trying to time the market, something that is tough for professional money managers to do with any success, let alone the average investor.

Sticking with the program does not guarantee profits, either. If a stock or mutual fund keeps going down, you are going to lose money. In general, you need at least three to five years of consistent investing to help even out the ups and downs and avoid being forced to sell in a falling market.

IX.

INSURANCE INSTRUMENTS AS INVESTMENTS

FOR purposes of accumulating retirement funds, it is hard to beat tax-favored 401(k)-type and IRA accounts. Before considering other ways to save for retirement, fund them to the fullest extent you can, especially if your employer matches your contributions.

After doing this, you may find it desirable—or even essential—to save even more for your retirement. Some of the investments you consider may have an insurance component. While insurance-based investment options can offer attractive tax advantages, they may also carry complicated restrictions, penalties, and expenses.

This chapter considers the basics of life insurance and of immediate and deferred annuities. An immediate annuity, as might be surmised, will start to yield an annual (or monthly) income to you soon after you purchase it. By contrast, deferred annuities will provide income only later. And deferred annuities come in two models: fixed and variable.

Deferred annuities in general, and variable annuities in particular, have been a source of considerable criticism in the last few years, because of their complexity and high fees. For reasons mentioned below, they give new life to the old maxim, "Never invest in something you don't understand."

Life Insurance

For most people, life insurance is best used only for the limited purpose of insuring your life. As noted earlier, a term life policy is usually the best choice because it is the least expensive. It is also easy to understand. Other types of life insurance, such as whole life and universal life, have an investment component. The good news is that these investments enjoy tax benefits. The bad news is that the investment returns are hard to measure and the policies often carry hidden high fees.

If you buy a policy with an investment component, the investment earnings will accumulate tax-free until withdrawn (and if they are eventually paid as part of the death benefit on the life of the insured, they are never taxed). However, there are tax penalties for withdrawals before age 59 ½, unless the policy holder is disabled or the withdrawal is taken as one of a series of substantially equal payments over his life expectancy, and insurance companies may levy their own charges for early withdrawals.

A larger problem with investment-type ("cash-value") life insurance is that it is difficult to figure what investment return you are earning. Part of your premium buys life insurance (which you may or may not need), and only part is invested. Insurance companies are less than helpful in disclosing what portion is invested, how much they are charging you for the life insurance component, and so forth. Figuring out whether you are getting a "good deal" on both your life insurance and your investment requires the analytical skills of an actuary. No doubt some cash-value policies earn respectable investment returns, but unless you can identify the rate of return, you are buying a pig in a poke.

Deferred Annuities

There are two basic types of annuities. Immediate annuities pay a stream of income to the investor beginning within a year of the date the policy is purchased or "annuitized." Deferred annuities do not provide income until at least a year, and usually many years, after the investment is made.

Deferred annuities are attractive primarily as a means of accumulating savings for retirement. Their chief advantage is that income taxes on investment earnings are deferred until the investor takes money out of the contract. However, as with most tax-favored accounts there are tax penalties for early withdrawals. In addition, and tax rules aside, most deferred annuities are subject to *surrender fees* if a policy is canceled after only a few years. These potential taxes and fees make deferred annuities suitable mainly for funds that an individual can afford to leave invested for the long term.

Deferred annuities may be purchased with a single (often large) premium or multiple premiums paid over a number of years. Multi-premium deferred annuities may have fixed or, more commonly, flexible premiums, *i.e.*, the investor contributes as much as he wants whenever he wants, much like investing in a mutual fund.

Flexible-premium annuities can, if they meet certain legal requirements, qualify as "individual retirement annuities" that are eligible for IRA contributions of up to $4,000 per year in 2006 and 2007 ($5,000 for individuals age 50 and older). "Qualified" IRA annuities offer the additional advantage that premiums may be deductible from taxable income, depending on your income level and participation in company pension plans.

However, as mentioned in the previous chapter, for tax reasons *it is usually not advisable to put IRA funds in a deferred annuity.* Like a belt worn with suspenders, the tax-deferral advantage of an annuity becomes redundant when the policy is held as an IRA. The IRA provides the same tax-deferral opportunity on its own, *without* any of the surrender fees that most annuities carry.

A good rule of thumb is to consider investing in a deferred annuity only after you have contributed as much as you can to a separate IRA and other tax-favored retirement plans such as 401(k), 403(b), and SEP plans. In this way, you will take full advantage of the deferral of income taxes on both contributions and investment earnings.

If you have additional capital to invest for the long term, an annuity will provide tax-deferred investment buildup. You will not be allowed to deduct your contribution, but there is no ceiling on how much you can contribute. If your employer does not offer a pension plan, deferred annuities may be a useful (if expensive) vehicle to accumulate savings for retirement.

The investment gains in a deferred annuity accumulate tax-free until the investor either takes withdrawals or until he annuitizes (converts the policy into a stream of income payments payable over his lifetime). During this accumulation period, the policyholder may elect to cancel the policy (surrender it) and receive a cash-surrender value as stipulated in the contract. Most contracts also allow partial withdrawals.

In either instance, surrender charges will be levied, typically ranging from five to ten percent of the policy's cash value. These charges usually are highest during the first year of the contract and typically are phased out over five to seven years, although this varies widely and a few policies levy charges as long as 12 years. Some multi-premium policies start the surrender-charge schedule over again each time you make a new payment. These policies, and policies with steep charges, should be avoided. *You should avoid deferred annuities altogether unless you expect to leave your funds invested long enough to avoid surrender charges.*

Deferred annuities provide for a refund to a designated beneficiary in the event the policyholder dies during the accumulation period. The refund usually is the cash value of the contract or the net sum of total contributions less withdrawals and charges, whichever is higher. It may be payable to the beneficiary in a lump sum or a series of annuity income payments payable over a few years or over the beneficiary's lifetime. The beneficiary also may have the option of leaving the money invested, where it will continue to grow tax free until it is withdrawn. Carefully read the options specified in the contract, as they will vary depending on whether the contract is jointly owned, who is named as the owner, whom the owner designates as a beneficiary, and whether the beneficiary is a spouse.

Deferred annuities may be either variable or fixed in their returns. We can consider variable annuities first. To be clear: A variable annuity is a deferred annuity where the investment return varies with market conditions and asset performance—and with account maintenance fees.

Variable Annuities

Variable annuities combine the investment opportunities of mutual funds with the tax-favored treatment of annuities. Like a mutual fund, the premiums paid into a variable annuity are invested in a fund chosen by the investor, and the investment return depends on how well the selected assets perform. Unlike regular mutual funds, the investment gains in a variable annuity accumulate tax-free until income payments begin or withdrawals are taken. Thus, variable annuities offer a potentially larger after-tax return than a comparable mutual fund. In recent years, mutual fund companies have aggressively marketed these policies as a tax-sheltered investment, and sales have soared.

The policyholder is given a selection of funds to choose from, similar to a family of mutual funds. These so-called "subaccounts" typically might include a bond fund, an income fund, a growth-oriented stock fund, an international stock or bond fund, and a money market fund. Many policies also offer one or more "fixed-rate" subaccounts that are similar to a traditional fixed-rate annuity (discussed in the next section). Once the investor allocates his funds among the available subaccounts, he can switch from one subaccount to another without incurring taxes.

The tax-sheltering advantage of a variable annuity must be weighed against some disadvantages. The fees charged to cover fund management expenses, administrative costs and the like run higher than on regular mutual funds. Add to this a separate charge for mortality risk, and total expenses can easily top two percent per year. There also may be an annual maintenance charge as high as $30. In addition, a few states levy a tax of as much as 3.5 percent on your premium payments. There may also be transfer fees when you switch from one subaccount to another, and restrictions on the number of switches you can make each year.

Unlike regular mutual funds, variable annuities also carry hefty *surrender charges* if you withdraw all or part of your investment in the early years of the contract. As noted earlier, these charges vary widely; on one policy we have seen they run as high as 12 percent and apply as long as 12 years. In addition, withdrawals taken before age 59 ½ also are subject to tax penalties similar to those levied on IRAs. In contrast, withdrawals from regular (non-IRA) mutual funds face no such penalty.

Taking these costs and lack of liquidity into account, some investors might be better off with a regular mutual fund. If you do not expect to leave your funds invested for at least 5 years, you almost surely should avoid variable annuities with surrender charges. If you do decide to invest, look for policies with annual expenses under 1.5 percent and a low annual contract charge (under $25). Annuities sold through discount brokerages and investment companies usually are less expensive than those sold by insurance agents and full-service stockbrokers, because their commission costs are lower. Companies that offer low-cost mutual funds, such as Vanguard and T. Rowe Price, usually sell variable annuities with comparably low expenses.

If you do invest, a variable annuity offers the greatest investment potential if you put your funds in a stock fund subaccount, since stocks historically have outperformed bonds over the long run. Many policyholders reportedly invest in money-market subaccounts, or in fixed-rate subaccounts earning a return that is fixed at a specific rate for six months, a year, or a few years. These fixed-rate subaccounts are less volatile, but their low yields are eaten away by management fees. In addition, the potential gains from tax-deferred compounding are smaller in a low-yielding subaccount. It is preferable to invest in a conservative stock fund comprised of stocks paying generous current yields.

Variable annuities provide investors with a way to earn higher returns than those provided by fixed-rate annuities (discussed below). However, the higher potential returns from stocks carry higher risks. To attract investors who are averse to investment risk, insurers offer various guarantees on variable annuities. The most common is a guaranteed minimum death benefit, which promises that the death benefit will never be less than a certain amount. That may equal the total premiums paid, or the value of the account on a selected "anniversary date," or the premiums plus a guaranteed return of five percent, etc. This guarantee is not free, however. Its cost is reflected in the policy's expense charges or, if the benefit is optional, as an additional expense equal to perhaps 0.15 percent of the account's value each year.

Some variable annuities guarantee "living benefits" as well. They may guarantee that the investor will never lose more than a given percentage of his premiums, or that he will get back at least his premiums or his premiums plus a fixed return. The cost of this benefit ranges from 0.75 to 1.5 percent of the account value each year. Other contracts charge 0.25 to 0.5 percent of the account to guarantee that the annuity will be convertible in the future to a minimum number of annuity income payments. As a rule, the more generous these and other guarantees are, the more expensive they are — and their total cost can quickly add up. The combined cost of purchasing all the available guaranteed benefits could cut the return on your variable annuity investment by more than two percentage points annually.

For these and other reasons, variable annuities remain controversial. They may make sense under specific conditions for sophisticated investors who know what technicalities to monitor in the contract. Unfortunately they have too often been aggressively marketed to people not in a position to understand the trade-offs involved. Finally, and as with a mutual fund investment, it is essential to check the performance record of the funds offered within a variable annuity.

Fixed-Rate Annuities

Until a few years ago, deferred annuities were marketed primarily as fixed-rate annuities. Although these now have been eclipsed by variable annuities, they still are available, primarily through insurance agents.

Unlike a variable annuity, the rate of return on a fixed-rate annuity depends on the interest rate credited to the invested funds by the insurance company. This interest rate is fixed for a period of time, usually a year, after which the company may readjust the rate and fix it for another limited period. This "current" rate, so called because it varies with the market level of interest rates and the company's financial position, is guaranteed by the company not to fall below a minimum rate, usually three to four percent, during the life of the policy. Each company has its own method for setting the current rate. Some offer very high rates for an initial "guarantee period," which may last several years, but there is no guarantee that their "renewal" rate credited after the guarantee period expires will be equally attractive.

Fixed annuities appeal to conservative investors because their rate of return is less volatile than that on variable annuities. However, the potential return also is lower, because the premiums for fixed annuities are invested conservatively by insurance companies in fixed-dollar claims, usually bonds. Most policies currently pay about their guaranteed minimum rate. Taking into consideration mortality charges and other ongoing expenses, the net rate of return is likely to be no more than the rate of price inflation plus a couple of percentage points, at best. If you take money out and trigger surrender fees, your returns will be even lower.

A more flexible alternative to the traditional fixed-rate annuity is the fixed-rate subaccount available as an option in many variable annuities. The rate of return usually is similar and is fixed by some companies for as long as three years, but the investor has the added advantage of being able to switch funds out of the fixed-rate subaccount into other, less conservative, subaccounts. In contrast, the only way to shift funds out of a traditional fixed-rate annuity is to surrender the policy, which may trigger surrender charges.

Some fixed-rate annuities offer the option of taking a loan against the value of the contract, which enables the policyholder to access his funds without cancelling the contract. This feature is less common on new policies, which usually allow partial withdrawals instead. As with any withdrawal, a loan will have tax consequences, possibly including penalties for early withdrawal. In addition, most companies will charge interest.

Tax Treatment of Deferred Annuities

The investment earnings on deferred annuities (whether fixed-rate or variable) are not taxed as income until the policyholder withdraws money or surrenders the contract. Withdrawals and surrenders before the annuity starting date are subject to income tax. The portion of any payment that counts as taxable income depends on (1) whether the policy is an IRA and (2) whether the investment was made before or after August 13, 1982.

If it is an IRA financed with deductible contributions, the full amount of any withdrawal is taxed. If it is a nondeductible IRA or simply a non-IRA annuity, the portion that represents investment earnings rather than a return of principal is taxed.

With respect to item (2), if you invested in a policy *after* August 13, 1982, the first withdrawals made before the annuity starting date are treated as investment earnings and are fully taxable. After all the investment earnings have been withdrawn, additional withdrawals are treated as a return of principal and are tax-free. (This treatment also applies to withdrawals that are attributable to investments made after August 13, 1982 in contracts that were purchased before August 14, 1982.) Also, loans from policies subject to this tax rule are treated as cash withdrawals and therefore may be taxable.

If you invested before August 14, 1982, the tax treatment is the exact opposite (and more favorable). The first withdrawals are treated as returns of the investor's capital and are tax-free; after the entire principal has been withdrawn, additional withdrawals are treated as taxable investment earnings. Loans from such policies are tax-free.

Taxable withdrawals are taxed as ordinary income at federal rates as high as 35 percent. This applies even to variable annuities, even though the income withdrawn from these may represent capital gains or qualified dividends that, if they came from a regular mutual fund, would be taxed at a top rate of only 15 percent. In effect, *an annuity converts capital gains and qualified dividend income into ordinary income*. Investors must balance the advantage of tax-deferred compounding within an annuity, against the more favorable treatment accorded to capital gains realized outside of an annuity. A variable annuity still may be suitable if you plan to seek investment buildup primarily through reinvested interest rather than unrealized capital gains.

To discourage investors from using policies for short-term tax sheltering, the IRS levies a tax penalty equal to 10 percent of the taxable portion of any withdrawal or surrender made before the policyholder reaches age 59 ½. The few exceptions to this penalty include payments received by a totally disabled person, payments received by a beneficiary or estate after the policyholder's death, and, notably, withdrawals that are part of a series of equal payments received over the life expectancy of the taxpayer or the joint life expectancies of the taxpayer and a beneficiary.

If a deferred annuity is held as an IRA, the policyholder may, without tax consequences, withdraw the entire investment and deposit it within 60 days, or "roll it over" directly, into another IRA or qualified retirement plan. Non-IRA annuities may be transferred tax-free to other annuity accounts (with the same insurance company or a different one), but this transfer should be done carefully, without the policyholder directly receiving any funds, so as to avoid taxation. (Ask the company to do a "1035 exchange.")

These tax-free options are useful if you find yourself stuck in an annuity earning poor returns, or if the financial position of your insurance company deteriorates. But beware: surrender fees can make such transfers costly during the early years of the policy.

A final tax consideration is the treatment of death benefits in the event the annuitant dies before the annuity starting date, *i.e.*, before beginning to receive annuity income. Death benefits in excess of premium payments — in other words, investment gains — are taxable to heirs as ordinary income. In contrast, the cost basis in regular investments usually is "stepped up" to the market value at the time of death—in other words, heirs pay no tax on investment gains that occurred before death.

This different tax treatment makes deferred annuities *unsuitable for accumulating assets to leave to heirs*. Here again, critics charge that the technicalities of variable annuities are too often ignored by sales people—and too easily misunderstood by investors who might wish to build an estate.

Immediate Annuities

To repeat, immediate annuities start to pay you a monthly or quarterly income within a year after you buy them. As such, they are not useful for accumulating a nest egg, but they are worth discussing to give you a better idea of their potential value down the road, after you retire.

Immediate annuities protect retirees against the risk of outliving their savings, by allowing them to convert those savings into a steady stream of income that lasts for as long as they live. In addition to providing financial security, annuities are attractive to retirees who want to maximize their monthly income, perhaps to supplement their Social Security benefits or pay for ongoing uninsured medical expenses.

Annuities are best suited to the circumstances of older people for two reasons: (1) older people are most likely to have accumulated sufficient funds to buy them, and (2) they are at an age at which the return on an annuity is most attractive. The income that you can obtain for a given premium increases with the age at which the annuity payments begin, because older individuals on average will live (and receive annuity income) for a shorter period than younger individuals.

For example, if a 65-year old man paid $100,000 for an annuity, he might receive an income of about $650 per month, based on the annuity income rates available in 2005. But if a 75-year old bought the same policy, his monthly income would be much larger, about $900.

Men can usually buy a larger annuity income for a given premium than women can, because the life expectancy for men is, on average, shorter than that for women. However, some insurance companies now use unisex mortality tables for men and women, with no provision for taking into account their different life expectancies. In other words, women and men of the same age get the same annuity income rates. Women will generally find it to their financial advantage to buy from a company offering these unisex policies. Men will find the opposite.

A large portion of annuity income usually is tax-free. This is because the income is partly a return *of* principal and partly a return *on* principal. Only the portion that represents investment earnings is taxable. However, the rules are different if you bought the annuity directly with funds from a deductible IRA or other tax-favored retirement account. In that case, you never paid income tax on either the original investment or the investment earnings in the IRA, so *all* of the annuity income is taxable.

Anyone considering an annuity must balance the security of a steady monthly income with the desire to bequest wealth. Remember, the insurance company wins the gamble when annuity holders die before the age determined by life expectancy tables. If someone receives annuity payments for only one or two years, then passes away unexpectedly, heirs would forfeit a substantial amount to the insurer (unless they have a type of policy that continues making payments after death). Also consider other sources of income. Someone with a steady stream of payments from a pension plan will probably need an annuity less than an individual who does not have a similarly reliable source of income.

Some critics of immediate annuities contend that most people would be better off holding onto their nest egg themselves, then taking periodic withdrawals roughly equal to payments they would get from an annuity.

They say that individuals using this strategy would retain both an income stream *and* the potential to leave heirs with a substantial account balance (or to have the balance available for other uses during retirement). The relative benefits of this strategy depend, to a great extent, on the returns an investor is able to achieve, as well as market conditions during the investment period. If you rely on your own schedule of withdrawals, there is no guarantee that the money will last for your whole lifetime. (If your investments perform poorly, the odds get worse.) Whatever their drawbacks, annuities do provide this assurance.

Recent research on the topic has found that in many situations, it is best to have both. In combination, an annuity *and* an investment account help assure a steady income throughout one's lifetime, while providing the potential for investment growth and fulfilling the desire to leave a bequest.

Hedging Against the Risk of Price Inflation

The dollar amount of the income you get from most immediate annuities is fixed. If you buy one at age 70 and it pays you $500 a month at that age, it will still pay $500 a month at age 85. There usually is no provision for cost-of-living adjustments. Thus the real (inflation-adjusted) income from the annuity decreases over time.

For example, suppose you had started receiving that $500 a month income in 1990. Taking into account price inflation since then, your income would have to be about $775 today in order for it to have the same purchasing power it had in 1990. And this was a period of relatively modest price inflation (2.8 percent a year, on average). If the rate of inflation increased, the purchasing power of the $500 would erode even faster.

One solution to this dilemma is to buy an inflation-adjusted annuity, whose monthly income is periodically increased to keep pace with price inflation. But these are very hard to find. In fact, we are aware of only one company that offers them, Vanguard (working with AIG Life Insurance). Moreover, the extra feature of inflation protection involves a trade-off: the initial monthly income is substantially lower than it is for an annuity without it. For example, a 75-year old male paying a $100,000 premium could currently get a monthly income of $943 on Vanguard's standard annuity. With the inflation-adjusted annuity, the income would be only $766 to start.

We have no connection with Vanguard and mention this product for reference only.

Down the Road: Coordinating Annuity Income with Investments

Many people will need to supplement Social Security and annuity income with investment income from other sources, such as a 401(k), an IRA, a

Roth IRA, or taxable savings accounts.

If you have more than one of these types of accounts available, you will need to decide which ones to draw down first. Your decision about which accounts to tap, and in what order, will depend on a number of factors. These include your age, how much money you want to withdraw, and the anticipated size of your estate.

In addition, tax considerations may also influence the order in which you take withdrawals.

If your primary concern is income (not your estate), you might wish to liquidate taxable accounts first. That way the money in tax-qualified retirement plans can grow tax deferred as long as possible.

For purposes of building an estate, however, you would probably take the opposite course. When estate taxes are more important to you than income considerations, you may wish to draw IRA and other retirement plan assets down first. Why? The stocks you leave to heirs in a taxable account can receive a step-up in valuation basis at your death. As noted earlier in this chapter, that will free your heirs from taxes on your capital gains.

Similarly, for estate planning, if you have both a Roth IRA and a regular IRA, it is often advisable to tap the regular IRA assets first. The heirs will not have to pay income tax on Roth IRA withdrawals, because a Roth IRA receives a step-up in valuation upon your death. By contrast, their withdrawals from your regular IRA will be subject to tax.

X.
SHOULD YOU USE A FINANCIAL ADVISOR?

ACCUMULATING a nest egg for retirement does not always translate into a desire or ability to invest it. If you do not feel confident about your investment abilities, you might consider hiring an investment professional to help your savings grow.

Anyone scouting out investment professionals needs to know more than just names and professional designations. While there are many worthy professionals out there, those who decide to seek professional assistance should expect to encounter an industry environment that, while it has generally changed for the better over the last few years, still bears the markings of a professional Wild West.

The fact is anyone can call himself a financial consultant, financial analyst, or wealth manager without registering with securities regulators or meeting any educational and experience requirements. Questionable practices can range from an overzealous enthusiasm for high-commission products, to investment recommendations that simply don't make sense (the two are often connected), to outright fraud.

Competence, honesty, and integrity vary widely among financial planners. Some are excellent, while others are outright crooks. And some have their own self-interest, rather than your financial future, at heart.

Separating the shining stars from the rotten apples might take some legwork, and don't become discouraged if your first few interviews don't click. It may take time to settle on someone with whom you feel comfortable divulging your most intimate financial secrets and entrusting your financial future. What follow are six suggestions to aid your search.

Think About What You Want a Financial Advisor To Do for You

Investment professionals offer a wide variety of services and products. To narrow the field, consider first how you wish to work with one, your own investment temperament and confidence in your investment abilities, and the kinds of services you want an advisor to perform.

Some people have no desire to manage their portfolios, and are happy to give someone else complete discretionary control over their assets. As long as they find the right people to handle their money, monitor their progress periodically, and feel comfortable with the reasoning behind their decisions, handing the investment reins to someone else makes sense for them.

An investment manager who works with clients on an ongoing basis—

perhaps one who is compensated based on a percentage of the value of the assets he or she manages—can be a logical choice here. If this arrangement seems right for you, discuss whether the advisor would work on a discretionary or non-discretionary basis. With non-discretionary accounts, a financial manager agrees to contact clients before making trades in an account. Under a discretionary arrangement, the advisor need not consult a client before making investment changes.

On the other hand, individuals who generally prefer to handle their own investments may not be very good candidates for ongoing investment management, either on a discretionary or non-discretionary basis. Yet they might still want to hire a financial advisor from time to time to coach them about specific events, such as a lump-sum distribution, or to conduct a "financial checkup" to make sure they haven't overlooked anything important.

In those cases, a professional who charges *an hourly consultation fee*, either on a one-time or periodic basis, may be appropriate. While such an individual might make investment, tax, or planning recommendations, the client will usually be responsible for actually carrying them out. Be aware, though, that while professions such as accountants or attorneys routinely work under hourly fee compensation arrangements, the majority of investment and financial planning professionals do not.

As you speak with financial advisors, a few may recommend a low or no-cost written financial plan to get a better view of your financial picture. While some may use the information you provide to craft a carefully-considered written plan and an effective, individualized investment program, others will produce an off-the-shelf computer-generated report that serves as little more than a starting point for a sales pitch.

Evaluate Compensation Arrangements

More commonly, financial advisors today are paid in one of two ways:

A commission on the investment products they sell you. A commissioned advisor is paid by the companies whose products he or she sells. To avoid the negative connotation of the word "commission," most advisors have expunged the term from their business cards. Instead, they may refer to themselves as "fee-based," which means they earn their living through a combination of fees and commissions. Typically, a fee-based advisor will charge a minimal fee for a written financial plan, then implement that plan with mutual funds and other products carrying a sales charge.

Advisors who work under a fee-based arrangement usually earn the lion's share of their living from sales commissions, and use the financial plan to get potential clients to "commit" to the process. Some will waive the fee if you later decide to implement the plan by investing through them. Others try to mask their compensation by selling products with "back-end" sales charges that kick in if you sell before a specified period of time. These products can be the most expensive for investors in the long run, and the advisor still gets a commission regardless of whether the sales charge is up-front or deferred.

A percentage of the value of the assets they manage for you. Most advisors working under this arrangement calculate compensation based on a percentage of assets under management. This type of compensation is not contingent on the sale of a particular product, and is therefore considered by many to be a more objective way to provide advice. Depending on the advisor's fee structure and the size of your account, it may be more cost-effective over the long-term than a commission-based arrangement.

As already noted, you may also come across professionals who work on an hourly basis, although they generally provide periodic advice to point you in the right direction, rather than ongoing investment management. Some advisors work through a salary and bonus paid by the employer. Financial advisors who work for banks, credit unions, or other organizations are usually paid a salary, but you will may pay a fee or commission to the employing institutions. A small but growing group work under a flat fee or retainer-type arrangements in which they agree to manage your money and perhaps provide some other services for a set annual fee.

There is a long-standing debate about which type of compensation arrangement is the most cost-effective and objective. Advisors who work on commission have the most incentive to push high-ticket products because they make higher commissions. The only question is whether or not they do it. While many investment professionals who work on commission are honest individuals who work in their clients' best interests, overzealous commission-hounds are still a very common breed. If you decide to use a commissioned advisor, make sure you understand all the fees you are paying.

Know What Professional Designations Really Mean

Having an alphabet soup of professional designations after someone's name might look impressive, but it is not necessarily a sign of professional accomplishment or competence. Certain professional designations require years of study, while others involve little more than paying membership dues every year.

Professional designations and credentials can provide valuable insight about an advisor's training. They may also provide some clues on the type of products or solutions someone is likely to recommend. An advisor with one or more professional designations that focus on insurance, for example, may lean toward insurance-based products and solutions.

The web site for the National Association of Securities Dealers (NASD), a professional organization for the brokerage industry, now lists more than 60 professional designations that their membership uses. Perhaps the most common of these is CFP (Certified Financial Planner). As a prerequisite to obtaining a CFP designation, candidates must have at least three years of personal financial planning experience and a bachelor's degree, or at least five years of personal financial planning experience. They must pass a final certification exam, and meet continuing education requirement of 30 hours over a two-year period.

Individuals who give investment advice and offer investment products such as mutual funds must submit a form to the Securities and Exchange Commission to use the letters RIA (Registered Investment Advisor) after their names. Contrary to appearances, this is a legal requirement rather than a professional designation.

For a list of other designations, what they mean, and the organizations that confer them, check the NASD web site at www.nsad.com. (Look for the section on "Understanding Investment Professional Designations.") You can confirm the professional designation of any individual by contacting the issuing organizations, which are also listed on this web site.

Get a Handle on Performance

One of the first questions many people ask a financial advisor is how well his or her investments have performed. It is also one of the trickiest to answer. Unlike money managers who work for pension funds or other institutional investors, financial advisors for individuals rarely have their performance audited by a third party. A common trick is to highlight the performance of their most successful accounts, while keeping the clinkers hidden in a drawer.

There are ways to cut through the clutter. A growing number of investment managers publish client newsletters with track record accounts and their historical performance. Reviewing those newsletters, especially those that go back several years, provides both a performance paper trail as well as valuable insight into how a portfolio responds under various market conditions. Other advisors use software that allows them to present their track records based on the aggregate performance of all accounts they manage.

Ask the investment manager about strategies behind the performance. Did a heavy investment in tech stocks cause the portfolios to skyrocket during the late 1990s, but tank in subsequent years? Or did a balanced approach keep things on a more even keel? Does the advisor have a strategy that emphasizes dividend-paying stocks, or does she prefer growth stocks that pay little or no dividends? If you have a taxable account, find out how the manager plans to minimize taxes.

Question any numbers that seem too good to be true. With the plunge in the stock market from early 2000 to 2004, many advisors consider themselves lucky if their equity portfolios broke even over the period. Those claiming annualized returns of 25 percent during those difficult times are either really skilled at picking stocks, or inflating claims.

Check out backgrounds. With an Internet connection and a little information, you need not hire a private investigator to find out if a financial advisor has a shady past. If you are considering working with a broker you should know about the Central Registration Depository (CRD), a computerized database that contains information about most brokers, their representatives, and the firms they work for. CRD information includes employment experience, educational backgrounds, and whether or not a broker has had any run-ins with regulators or has received serious complaints from investors. The NASD's Public Disclosure Program provides CRD information free of charge. You can obtain disclosure reports through the NASD website or by calling 1-800-289-9999.

Investment advisors who manage $25 million or more in client assets must register with the SEC, which houses information about them in its Investment Adviser Registration Depository (IARD). To find out about advisors, read their registration forms, called the "Form ADV." Part 1 of the form has information about the advisor's business and any problems with clients or regulators. Part 2 outlines services, fees, and strategies. You can obtain copies of Form ADV from the advisor you are considering, or from the investor information section of the SEC's website (www.sec.gov).

Investment advisors who manage less than $25 million must generally register with the state securities agency in the state where they have their principal place of business. For a list of state securities regulators and contact information, visit the web site for the North American Securities Administrators Association at www.nasaa.org.

Watch for Red Flags

As you interview candidates, watch for these red flags that the Securities and Exchange Commission says could indicate trouble ahead:

- Recommendations from a sales representative based on "inside" or "confidential" information, such as an upcoming research report or a prospective merger.

- Representations of a spectacular profit over a short period of time.

- A recommendation that you make a dramatic change in your investment strategy, such as moving from low risk investments to speculative securities, or concentrating your investments exclusively in a single product.

- Switching your investment in a mutual fund to a different fund with the same or similar objective, which may simply be an attempt to generate additional commissions.

- A recommendation to trade the account in a manner that is inconsistent with your investment goals and the risk you want or can afford to take.

Consider Starting Slowly

Unless you are already feel very comfortable with an investment manager there is no reason to sign over your life's savings if you'd prefer to work your way into a professional relationship gradually. Start with the smaller stake, perhaps as little as the advisor's required minimum account size. You can always add to the account later as you gain confidence and build trust. Another option might be to begin with a non-discretionary account that requires the advisor to contact you before making a trade. Once you feel comfortable with an advisor's investment moves, you can switch to a discretionary account.

Finally, remember that the mark of a worthy investment manager is a strategy that has withstood the test of time in bull and bear markets, and that, when implemented consistently, can help you reach your goals over the long term. It is not someone who nudges clients into high-cost products they don't understand, promises spectacular short-term returns, or implements cookie-cutter strategies regardless of their clients' risk profiles or financial goals.

APPENDIX A

"PENSION REFORM" AND THE VANISHING OF THE TRADITIONAL PENSION IN THE PRIVATE SECTOR

A S noted in Chapter V, in August 2006 President Bush signed into law the Pension Protection Act of 2006, a major pension reform bill. The new law represents the latest act in a drama that began more than three decades earlier, in 1974, with the passage of the Employee Retirement Income Security Act. ERISA was a pension-reform law intended to address a variety of weaknesses, inconsistencies, and perceived defects in the way companies were offering and administering their pension plans. In retrospect, it can be seen as the first step in a long regulatory process that unintentionally contributed to the traditional pension's demise.

Early Efforts at Reform

The original objective of pension plans was to provide a stable, secure income for retirees. However, as the first large wave of beneficiaries reached retirement age in the 1950s and 1960s, a number of difficulties became evident. In those days, existing pension laws were intended mainly to prevent company sponsors from claiming excessive tax deductions for their contributions to pension funds. There were no regulations concerning participation, vesting, funding or fiduciary standards.

In several cases that received wide publicity, workers lost their promised benefits because companies went out of business and were unable to make payments, or because eligibility rules for pension plans were exceedingly stringent or had not been described clearly to workers. In other instances, pension funds had been mismanaged and invested for the benefit of the employer or individuals rather than employees. Many plans were *underfunded*, *i.e.*, the value of current pension fund assets was less than the present value of benefits owed to past and present employees.

In response to increasing complaints about such abuses, Congressional hearings were held, and in 1974 Congress legislated ERISA (profiled in the box on the next page). It was intended to ensure that private pension plans were adequately funded and that participation and vesting requirements were reasonable. A key feature was the creation of the Pension Benefit Guaranty Corporation (PBGC). This was to be an independent Government agency, created to ensure that workers would receive a guaranteed level of pension benefits even if an employer went out of business or a pension plan became insolvent.

In a classic example of unintended consequences, the ERISA law, rather than solving such problems, actually created new ones. True, some plans

111

were amended to comply with the standards as intended by the law's framers. However, ERISA had contrary effects as well. The costs and complications of complying with the new law forced many smaller funds to terminate, presumably at a cost to covered employees.

Plans that were poorly funded prior to the enactment of the new laws soon became a liability to Federal taxpayers. Indeed, some mismanaged plans were terminated before ERISA even went into effect—and all ob-

---

The Employee Retirement Income Security Act of 1974
(ERISA)

ERISA provides for the following:

1. If an employer chooses to have a pension plan, the employer must submit annual financial reports to covered employees and to the Secretary of Labor; and, upon request of a covered employee, a statement of his or her total nonforfeitable benefits.

2. The employer must provide full vesting by one of the vesting plans specified in the law. (The 1986 tax reform bill amended this provision, effectively speeding up vesting schedules.)

3. Upon leaving employment, an employee paid vested pension benefits must have the option of investing the benefits in an Individual Retirement Account (IRA) within 60 days of such payment; or, with the consent of a new employer, reinvesting such assets from the previous plan into the new employer's plan.

4. Funding of pensions by employers is required to be accomplished over a period of up to 40 years, on a straight-line basis. Failure to provide the minimum funding requirements will lead to assessment of penalties (sometimes severe) against such employers.

5. The Pension Benefit Guaranty Corporation (PBGC) was established in order to guarantee the payment of a minimum level of vested benefits if a terminated plan had insufficient assets to pay those benefits. The PBGC was to be funded with mandatory premiums collected from employers, and to finance benefits was authorized to claim up to 30 percent (this level has recently been increased) of the net worth of a company whose pension plan was terminated. The Labor Secretary is authorized to terminate plans that do not meet funding standards or are unable to pay benefits. Defined-contribution plans are, by definition, always fully funded, and thus are exempt from minimum funding rules and coverage by the PBGC.

6. ERISA's imposed fiduciary standards — such as the "prudent man" rule — for any person involved with the control, management, or disposition of a pension fund's assets.

ERISA does *not* oblige an employer to offer a pension plan. It applies only to private plans, and thus Federal, state, and local government plans are exempt from its provisions.

---

ligations to employees dissolved. Others remained underfunded, which sometimes meant that eventually they became the liability of the newly created PBGC.

ERISA tended to discourage the formation of new defined-benefit pension plans. Within a few years, 401(k) accounts would come into extensive use, and for a variety of reasons they proved more attractive to employers. In the meantime, an anomaly in ERISA added to the incentives for employers to terminate even fully funded pension plans.

Overfunded? Close Your Plan

In addition to encouraging underfunded plans to terminate and transfer the costs of pension financing to the Government, ERISA regulations have had other unintended consequences. In particular, they have encouraged the termination of "overfunded plans" and discouraged many employers from offering any pension coverage at all.

The financial bull market of the 1980s and 1990s led to tremendous increases in pension fund assets, from $210 billion in 1974 to far larger sums. One consequence of the unexpectedly high rate of appreciation in asset values was that a number of pension funds became "overfunded." (An overfunded plan is one with a surplus of assets over total benefit liabilities.)

ERISA regulations provided a strong incentive for employers to terminate overfunded plans. Why? Perversely, the *only* way an employer could legally tap into a surplus fund was to cancel the entire pension plan and pay off the present value of benefits owed to past and present employees. The employer could provide a new pension plan as a replacement — but was under no obligation to do so. Beyond the value of vested benefits, employees could be left with nothing.

As might be expected, employers terminated hundreds of plans in the 1980s solely to access surplus funds._

Mounting Deficits at the PBGC after 2001

The PBGC was intended to be a self-financing government-owned corporation, which would act as an insurer of private defined-benefit pension plans. Premiums paid by sponsors of defined-benefit plans to the agency were expected to be sufficient to cover the agency's costs of taking over and financing weak plans unable to meet benefit obligations.

Since its formation, however, the liabilities of the PBGC have often exceeded its assets. Various pension plans have become underfunded due to a combination of factors, including increasing pension costs as workers retire, and the inability of failing businesses to meet funding obligations. Some of these plans have been taken over by the PBGC.

During the 1980s and 1990s, the main source of PBGC liabilities was pension plans in declining industries, notably steel. Liabilities mushroomed after 2001 because low interest rates and erratic stock market returns raised pension liabilities, while a number of airlines approached or entered bankruptcy. The climax thus far, as can be seen in the table below, came in 2005, when the PBGC reached a settlement with United Airlines over the termination of the company's defined-benefit pension plans. Under the terms of the agreement, the PBGC will cover some $7 billion of the $9.8 billion the company owes in retirement benefits.

Competitive pressure in the airline industry could cause more airlines to declare bankruptcy and transfer their pension obligations to the PBGC. In September 2006, for example, a federal judge gave the go-ahead to Delta Airlines to turn over what could prove to be an even larger liability than United's to the PBGC. In the meantime, General Motors (and its parts-supplier, Delphi) and Ford are also struggling, in part because of the enormous and growing cost of paying pensions and retiree health benefits. (In reference to this burden, General Motors has sometimes been described as "a pension fund that makes cars on the side.") This raises the possibility of further huge pension transfers to the PBGC.

In short, the annual losses to the PBGC in recent years have been in the billions. In 2004, for example, it collected only $1.5 billion in premiums

The 10 Firms Presenting the Largest Pension Claims to the Pension Benefit Guaranty Corporation (PBGC), 1975-2005

Firm	Year	Claims
1. United Airlines	2005	$7.1 billion
2. Bethlehem Steel	2003	3.7 billion
3. U.S. Airways	2003, 2005	2.9 billion
4. LTV Steel	2002, 2003, 2004	2.0 billion
5. National Steel	2003	1.2 billion
6. Pan American Air	1991, 1992	841 million
7. Weirton Steel	2004	690 million
8. Trans World Airlines	2001	668 million
9. Kemper Insurance	2005	566 million
10. Kaiser Aluminum	2004	566 million
Top 10 Total		20.1 billion
Total, All Claims to PBGC		31.7 billion

Note: Amounts are listed in current dollars and are subject to revision. Source: PBGC, *Pension Insurance Data Book 2005*, online at pbgc.gov.

from employers and other pension sponsors; but it paid out more than $3 billion in benefit payments. The difference, $1.5 billion, had to be covered by the PBGC's assets.

The PBGC has billions in assets, consisting of the annual premiums it collects and the assets of the pension funds it has taken over. It also has billions in liabilities—the estimated value of the stream of future benefits promised to retirees covered by those plans *and* by plans it deems likely to default. Its *net asset position* is the difference between its assets and liabilities. As a result of recent plan terminations, the PBGC's net asset position declined from a surplus of $7.7 billion at the end of fiscal year 2001 to a deficit of $23 billion by the end of 2005. The agency's attempts to improve its balance sheet by increasing the premiums paid by employers have proven largely ineffective.

Not surprisingly, the PBGC's budgetary problems loomed large in the design of the Pension Protection Act of 2006. Perhaps the main initiative to shore up the PBGC's finances was to allow companies seven years from the time the new law takes hold in 2008 to attain 100-percent funding of their pension liabilities. (By comparison, the requirement in the past had been 90-percent funding.) The most troubled airlines were given extra time (17 years, or in a few cases 10) to reach full funding for their pension obligations.

In any case, there is no immediate threat of a liquidity crisis. The PBGC has the resources to pay the pension benefits owed to retirees covered by the plans it has acquired. What remains a threat, however, is that additional large companies may try to unload their pension commitments (perhaps invoking bankruptcy as the alternative, as United's negotiators have).

PBGC keeps track of such problem plans, and the estimated price tag if they all revert to the agency is a liability amount of more than $100 billion. It is this worst-case scenario that would trigger a big jump in annual benefit payments—and the possibility that taxpayers might wind up with the bill, as in the savings-and-loan bailout of the 1980s.

Cash-Balance Plans

As a separate issue, another key feature of the Pension Protection Act of 2006 was a template for how companies can initiate (or convert to) so-called "cash-balance" plans. Partly for the controversy surrounding them (on the grounds of possible discrimination against older workers) but also because they are likely to spread rapidly in the next few years, a brief note on them is in order here.

A cash-balance plan is a hybrid that combines features of defined-ben-

115

efit pensions and 401(k)-type accounts. The effect is to give the employer more certainty as to what liabilities are being incurred for pensions. But, particularly for those nearing retirement, a conversion by the employer from a traditional pension to a cash-balance plan is likely to reduce workers' pension benefits.

Perhaps one-third of private-sector workers with traditional pensions (defined-benefit plans) have already seen their employers convert them into cash-balance plans. That shift is now expected to accelerate. First, the 2006 pension reform law's 100-percent funding requirement has made traditional pensions more expensive to employers. Second, the 2006 law itself clarifies how employers can legally manage the conversion from the older to the newer type of plan. Third, in the same month the 2006 act was signed into law, a federal appeals court judge ruled that IBM's 1997 shift to a cash-balance plan did not discriminate against older workers, in effect giving other large companies a green light.

Under a cash-balance plan, a worker has a hypothetical account the company credits each year, typically in the amount of, say, three percent of annual pay, plus interest. Upon changing jobs or retiring, the employee can cash out the account balance or roll it into an IRA. One feature here is that the amount piling up (hypothetically) in the account is always known, not subject to the slings and arrows of market conditions, as in a traditional pension plan. Another consideration is that these plans, because of the way they are structured, usually work more to the advantage of younger workers than older ones.

In an update to reflect the terms of the Pension Protection Act of 2006, the Department of Labor draws *a distinction between cash-balance plans and 401(k)s.* The first retains defined benefits, while the second features defined contributions. Here are other differences the Department highlights:

- "Participation. Participation in typical cash balance plans generally does not depend on the worker's contributing part of their compensation to the plan…

- Investment Risks. The investments of cash balance plans are managed by the employer…. By contrast…Under 401(k) plans, participants bear the risks and rewards of investment choices.

- Life Annuities. Unlike many 401(k) plans, cash balance plans are required to offer employees the ability to receive their benefits in the form of lifetime annuities.

- Federal Guarantee. Since they are defined benefit plans, the benefits promised by cash balance plans are usually insured by…the PBGC.

…Defined contribution plans, including 401(k) plans, are not insured by the PBGC."

While such comparisons may seem technical, they will matter to employees of companies rearranging or terminating their plans. A case in point is IBM itself, which, as noted earlier, converted traditional pension arrangements to a cash-balance plan in 1997. (This is the plan the court ruled does not discriminate against older workers.) In January 2005, IBM blocked the cash-balance plan for future new employees. In January 2006 it froze the plan for all workers, effective at the end of 2007. From now on, the company will augment its contributions to 401(k) accounts. But it will end any future contributions to defined-benefit plans for its workers. Similar freezes have recently been imposed by Sears and Verizon.

Between these moves by blue-chip companies and the new rules favoring 401(k)-type accounts in the Pension Protection Act of 2006, it is perhaps understandable why some observers have declared this era "the age of the 401(k)."

Outlook

Every attempt by Congress to reform traditional pensions has made such plans more burdensome and less attractive to employers, who have often responded by terminating them outright. The losers may be employees themselves, who now have more options—but less income they can count on in retirement.

In response to the new Pension Protection Act, observers suggest that while there will still be a fortunate minority *receiving* traditional pension benefits in retirement 10 years from now, hardly any private-sector employees remaining at work will participate in a traditional, defined-benefit plan. More optimistically, others suggest that cash-balance plans may step in to recreate some of the predictability of the vanishing defined-benefit plans.

Notice, in any case, that we are talking only about private-sector workers. Appendix B shows that government employees at all levels experience a very different, and considerably more generous, pension environment.

117

APPENDIX B
PENSION PLANS FOR GOVERNMENT EMPLOYEES

T RADITIONAL pensions continue to flourish (if that is the word) as a desirable perquisite for government employees. As the chart on the next page shows, some 80 percent of government employees responding to a 2003 survey said their main retirement plan was a traditional, defined-benefit pension. This contrasted with under 30 percent of respondents in the private sector.

With about $3.5 trillion in assets, public-sector retirement accounts surpassed one-fourth of the total for the public and private sector combined in 2004. As noted in Chapter V, federal retirement accounts held about $1 trillion (or 8 percent of the $13.3 trillion total), while state and local accounts held over $2.5 trillion, or 19 percent of the total.

Government-sponsored pensions at the federal, state, and local levels do not operate under the same legal and financial constraints as for private businesses. Public plans are not subject to the same funding regulations as in the private sector, and political pressures can make voluntary funding lag.

In a telling historical footnote, in 1994 a group defining acceptable accounting standards regarding pensions gave carte blanche to state and local governments. The director of the group was so appalled that he wrote a ten page dissenting note. He contended that the absence of a clear set of guidelines comparable to those for the private sector was an invitation for state and local governments to finagle the books. In practice, his fears have been borne out in the interim, not typically by deception (although that does happen), but by widespread tendencies to neglect funding of pension obligations.

At the same time, generous pension benefits are a particularly attractive alternative to direct wage compensation, because *they require no immediate expenditure of tax revenue*. It is cheaper for public officials to promise a pension benefit than to give a raise, because the bill for the pension benefit will not come due until many years later. Traditionally, then, public employees have tended to receive better pensions than their counterparts in private industry. When benefits eventually fall due, the government's ability to finance such benefits is limited only by its ability to raise taxes or (at the federal level) borrow money.

In sum, because the incentives to grant generous benefits are so strong, and the incentives (both political and legal) to finance them so weak, public-sector pensions tend to be generous—and poorly funded. To put it more vividly, when a police officer or firefighter or someone in the military retires at 45 with as much as 75 percent of full salary, someone has to pay for the stream of pension benefits that may last the next 30 years or 40 years. Add the customary retirement health benefits and the price tag can be impressive.

Unlike the sea change in private-sector retirement plans, however, there has been no coherent or coordinated attempt to shore up funding practices for public-sector pensions. The result of this drift is virtually certain to be higher state and local taxes when the bills come due.

Federal Pensions

Federal (non-military) employees are covered by two pension plans. The Civil Service Retirement System (CSRS) covers employees hired before 1984, and the Federal Employees' Retirement System (FERS) covers employees hired after 1983 and anyone who opted to switch out of the CSRS plan. The CSRS plan is a defined-benefit pension that relies primarily on current taxpayer dollars to pay benefits to retirees.

The FERS plan is a three-tiered plan that combines Social Security benefits (with the employer share funded by taxpayer dollars) with an additional pension benefit (funded entirely by taxpayers) and a thrift savings plan financed by employee contributions. This latter component is a 401(k)-type

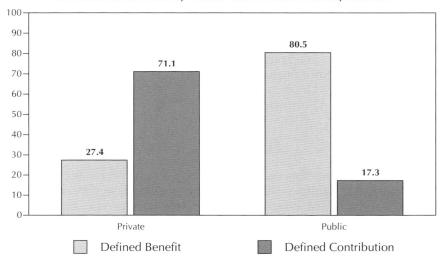

Chart 1B
Percentage of Participants Whose Primary Plan is Defined-Benefit or Defined-Contribution, Private and Public Sectors, in 2003

Source: Employment Benefits Research Institute.

119

arrangement, known as a 457 plan, introduced in 1997.

A third major Federal retirement program is the Military Retirement System (MRS). As with the earlier CSRS plan, there are no "accounts" building up to provide for military retirement benefits. They come straight from taxpayer dollars.

The number of Federal civilian employees covered has remained steady in recent years, at about 2.7 million. With the addition of the 457 plan, a majority of federal civil-service employees now have 401(k)-type accounts. In 2002 (the most recent year available), employee contributions to such 457 or Thrift Savings Plan accounts totaled $12 billion, as compared with $44 billion in federal government contributions.

Price inflation poses less of a threat to public-sector retirees than to retirees dependent on fixed-dollar retirement income. Both the MRS and CSRS plans feature benefits that are fully indexed to price inflation. By the same token, this feature, which is not available in most private-sector pensions, adds greatly to the *real cost* of these plans; it cannot be inflated away over the years.

State and Local Pensions

In any case, more attention has gone recently to the state-local tiers, notably to some city governments that have failed to fund fully their pension commitments. The concern, once gain, is that such temporizing reduces tax levels today, but will raise them tomorrow. The nub of the problem is that *the longer full funding is postponed, the less opportunity there is for funds placed in investment accounts today to grow at compound rates of growth over time.*

Unlike the federal government, state and local governments must balance their budgets (a requirement in most state constitutions). While such requirements would seem to limit in their capacity to finance pension benefits by running deficits and borrowing money, much depends on the "sincerity" or good faith behind accounting methods and budget details. In any case, these plans are not subject to federal pension regulation, and the degree of funding can vary greatly, from fully funded to pay-as-you-go.

Some governments have adequately funded their pensions only after sky-rocketing benefit liabilities threatened fiscal disaster, as in the case of New York City in 1974. That debacle found the City placed in receivership, with outside overseers coming in to oversee its finances for years to come.

Chicanery in San Diego

More recently, a comparable pension crisis has taken center stage in San

120

Diego. That city's municipal pension plan is in deficit to the tune of $1.4 billion—a sizable amount for a city San Diego's size. In itself the shortfall might seem only a technical setback. But investigators under the leadership of Arthur Leavitt, former head of the S.E.C., were called in only after a whistle blower inside the city's government sounded an alarm. Leavitt and his team contend that city officials consciously tried to mislead the press and public about the problem. These officials are accused of using accounting tricks to fudge the books (in a municipal version of Enron), and some may face prison as a result. Now a remedial catch-up plan is moving ahead full-throttle. But the gap remains: What services in the city budget should be cut to allow for the catch-up pension funding? Or should taxes be increased instead?

San Diego is just one city, perhaps an extreme case. Still, a 2006 Standard & Poor's study found declining adequacy of pension funding of the 20 largest American cities generally. Nearly all had experienced a drop in funding adequacy between 2000 and 2004 or 2005 (the endpoint depended on data availability). In the earlier year, booming financial markets had helped the 20 cities attain an average "funding adequacy ratio" of almost 100 percent. In other words, their estimated future pension liabilities were covered by adequate annual budget allocations into the appropriate accounts, and by favorable market returns on their investments.

Since then, a number of factors have either increased future pension liabilities or reduced their funding or both. As a result the 20-city average has fallen to only 84 percent funding adequacy—and an average underfunding estimate of about $1 billion per city. It is true that some part of the decline can be explained by transitory factors, such as the fall in the stock market after 2000 and the impact of low interest rates on the present value of future liabilities (pension liabilities usually rise when interest rates fall).

Still, even an optimist might wonder about the specific figures for some of the laggard cities. Hard-pressed Philadelphia floundered with barely 50 percent coverage. But Boston and Chicago did only a little better, at 63 and 65 percent. In Boston, for example, the Standard and Poor's study noted that "An unfunded pension liability that has grown to $2.1 billion in 2005 from $1.1 billion in 2000 has required the city to step up contributions…. Pension costs increased a significant $39.7 million, or 27.1 percent, in Boston's current budget due to an updated pension-funding schedule."

New York City: A Good Place to Work

Then there is New York City redux. Despite the appearance of probity, doubts have been raised about the accuracy of the City's published funding ratio for its pensions. While city officials contend that the City's pension plans have been fully funded in recent years, outside experts have a sharply different view—namely, that such conclusions are not based on generally accepted accounting practices. Indeed, even the City's own chief actuary has offered an alternate measure more in tune with generally accepted accounting practices that finds a funding ratio of only about 62 percent, and a shortfall of as much as $49 billion.

Unfortunately, state officials (notably including the governor) had accepted at face value the City's claim of full funding in recent years. On that shaky basis they proceeded to sweeten the pension terms for City workers—despite pleas from City officials not to. In an unholy "end around," municipal unions, turned down by the mayor when they requested pension privileges that went far beyond negotiated contracts with the city, went to Albany instead. There they reportedly pledged lavish campaign contributions to legislators and the governor. In response, the governor and the legislature imposed costly new guidelines upon New York City, leaving the City to pay the higher tab.

The result is that New York City school teachers received pension increases equal to 20 percent of their salaries in 2005. For police the benefits surpassed 40 percent, and for fire fighters, 60 percent. City employees have thus received large pension increases at the same time that the pension benefits of private-sector workers have continued to erode.

Storm Clouds?

Despite these and other increases, the controversial formula under which New York City's funding adequacy is measured continues to show that pension liabilities remain fully funded. Other formulas suggest otherwise. To be sure, there is no consensus among pension actuaries on the best way to measure funding adequacy, and the various yardsticks each have their technical strengths and weaknesses.

Still, one argument that holds no water is, "We'll pay for it when the time comes," to paraphrase a spokesperson for an organization of state and local governments. Setting aside arguments over accounting technicalities, the logic favoring *full funding* is compelling: Put the funds aside today, from today's tax revenue, and let the account balances benefit from compound growth rates over time. Otherwise, it will cost much more tax revenue when the time comes to pay out the pension benefits.

The episodes sketched out here are symptoms of a lack of rigorous and professional standards for measuring public-sector pension funding. Commenting on states such as Colorado, Illinois, and New Jersey, Lance Weiss (an actuary with a national accounting firm) observed, "There's no oversight; there's no requirements; there's no enforcement" when it comes to state and local pensions. More generally, Barclay's Global Investments has calculated that if such pension plans were held up to the same accounting standards as private companies, their pension liabilities with a present value of $2.5 trillion would be matched by only $1.7 trillion in current funding.[1]

Generalizing, a *New York Times* editorial written in August 2006 makes a larger point about shaky math and budgetary reckoning. It suggests that the New York City episode can serve as "a useful harbinger of the coming financial storm for governments, local, state and federal."

---

[1] As quoted by Mary Williams Walsh, "Public Pension Funds Face Billions in Shortages," *The New York Times*, August 8, 2006.

To buy publications or find out more about
American Institute for Economic Research contact us at:

American Institute for Economic Research

250 Division Street

Post Office Box 1000

Great Barrington, MA 01230

Phone: (413) 528-1216

Fax: (413) 528-0103

E-mail: aierpubs@aier.org

On-line: www.aier.org